LOVE IS MY RELIGION

VOLUME 2

LOVE IS MY RELIGION

VOLUME 2

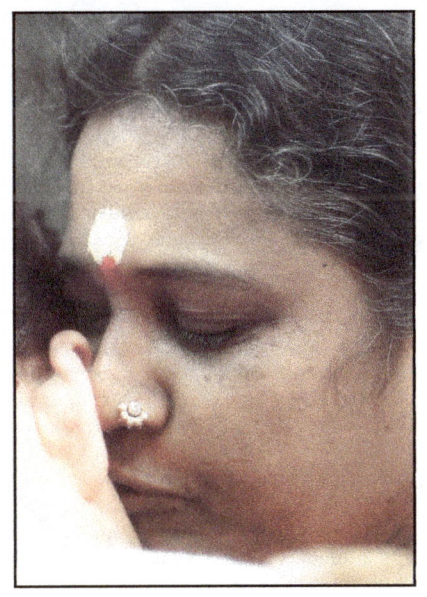

MATA AMRITANANDAMAYI
COMPILED BY JANINE CANAN MD

Love Is My Religion by Mata Amritanandamayi
compiled by Janine Canan MD
Copyright © 2019 by Mata Amritanandamayi Center
All rights reserved.
Except for the Introduction by Janine Canan, or for brief review,
no portion of this book may be reproduced, stored in a retrieval system,
transmitted in any form or by any means, or translated into any language,
without the written permission of the publisher.

Quotations in this book have been compiled from books, pamphlets, magazines,
films and songs published by Mata Amritanandamayi Math, India,
and Mata Amritanandamayi Center, USA;
from the web site www.Amritapuri.org, Amma's public talks and comments,
interviews and remarks to the editor.

Published by Mata Amritanandamayi Center
P.O. Box 613, San Ramon, California 95483
United States of America
www.amma.org
www.theammashop.org

First Printing: January, 2020

ISBN-13: 978-1-68037-870-2

CONTENTS

9. The Heart of Religion — 8

10. World Peace — 40

11. Overcoming Anger — 84

12. Good Qualities — 108

13. Quiet Mind — 158

14. Discrimination — 200

15. Detachment — 220

*Photographs of Sri Mata Amritanandamayi
cover, title page, 6.*

THE HEART OF RELIGION

God is all pervading, all powerful
and all knowing.

God pervades everything—all beings and things.

God does not live in some heavenly realm
but in all living creatures, moving and unmoving.

What we see in all of God's many different forms is God.

God is not a finite being, seated on a golden throne somewhere in the clouds,
but the pure Consciousness inherent in everything.

**Consciousness
is God.**

Like space, God is everywhere.

God is everything — is there anything that is not God?

**The human body is the seat of God-Consciousness.
Every creature is a house of God.
The ancient seers saw the whole universe as God's form.**

If everything is full of God, then what is not to be worshipped?

**God is One, but people worship God in a multiplicity of forms
according to their customs and beliefs.**

Christians say Christ, Muslims say Allah, Hindus say Krishna, Shiva, Devi —
but all refer to the same God.

One supreme Truth shines through all religions.

In Hinduism there is no such thing as separate religions.
From the viewpoint of our ancient visionaries, all are children of God.

The religious vision of the eternal Way is all-embracing.
The various religions are seen as alternate paths to the same destination.

The goal of human striving is to know the supreme Power
that illumines the Sun, the Moon and the stars.

The universe is far too complex to be explained by any single religion or philosophy.

It is wrong to force everyone to follow the same religious conventions.
Although the destination is ultimately the same for everyone,
the right path depends on one's point of departure.

In reality God is formless, but since people need form there are many paths to God.
We should choose the one we are most comfortable with and look within.

Ordinary people, whose intellects are not cultivated, cannot comprehend
God's formless, nameless nature, and so need a person or thing
to hold onto and open their hearts to.

Being imperfect we cannot be satisfied with others who are imperfect.
We keep searching, consciously or unconsciously, for an infinite universal Person
to whom we can unburden our sorrows — and so find some peace.

When Indians worship Rama, Krishna or Christ,
we are worshipping the eternal ideals that manifested through these incarnations.

As mere individuals they would not have been worshipped.
In a divine Person it is the omnipresent cosmic Intelligence we worship —
the supreme Truth.

Divine Consciousness exists everywhere —
It pervades everything and has neither inside nor outside.
But our individual identity — our sense of I — makes us perceive things
either as inside or outside of us.
When we turn our minds outward we become attached to outer things
and cling to the notion of mine.
The purpose of image worship is to draw the mind inward
and awaken the divine Consciousness within.

We are free to worship God in any form we wish —
Mother, Father, Guru, Friend, Lord, Lady, Child.
But whatever form we choose it is important to follow spiritual principles.

Through worship we cultivate an attitude that enables us
to love, honor and serve everything as innately divine.
As we become more aware that we and everything around us are God,
we develop an attitude of profound, all-inclusive acceptance.

The highest form of human relationship
is the relationship between the mother and the child.
A child is allowed to coax its mother with determination and tears,
and even when spanked still clings to her for consolation and protection.
This is the attitude we should have toward God.

For the mind to expand as wide as the universe, we need the attitude of a child.

Behold the pleasure with which children observe the world.
Everything is new in their eyes.
Their hearts are fresh, full of Love and beauty.
Everything gives them such joy!

Children have no worries or problems —
that is why we remember childhood so fondly and long to return to it.
Within each of us is an innocent playful child.

As we get older we lose our enthusiasm and joy and become dry and unhappy.
Why? Because we have lost our childlike innocence and faith.
But somewhere inside us a child's joy still lies dormant.
We need to rediscover it!

As we age and start losing our enthusiasm and happiness,
it is good to spend time with children
who can teach us to believe, love and play again —
who can show us how to smile from our hearts
and regain our look of wonderment.

The childlike innocence deep within us is God.

The innocence hidden deep within us is rediscovered as we go deeper
and deeper into our spiritual practices.
When we finally reach the ground of Consciousness
we will find our lost innocence, wonder and joy.

Children, God dwells deep in our hearts as innocent, childlike Love —
however veiled by constant self-centered thoughts and feelings.
Our innocence is always there, even when forgotten.
If we go deep into ourselves, we will rediscover and remember it.
For Love and wonder to come back, try to remember how you used to play.

Our innocent pure heart can save us.

To be close to God, try to be like a child whose world is full of wonder,
imagination, play and Love.

Try to awaken the attitude of a child and you will be able to learn and grow.

Children, once innocence awakens in our hearts
and we can see everything in that light,
there is nothing but Bliss.

The source of Bliss is within us — we can access it any time we want.

God is the principle of Life, the inner light of Consciousness and pure Bliss.

To experience This, open your heart like a flower spreading out its petals.
God's grace is the Sun that shines upon everything.

Open the door of your heart and let in the Light.

The Mother of the Universe,
who is its cause, sustenance and dissolution,
loves her Creation with a selfless Love that flows equally to all creatures.
The world and its divine founding Power are inseparable

as Sun and light, honey and sweetness, lute and sound, word and meaning.
Everything we perceive in this world is simply one of her
many moods and manifestations.

You may wonder why Amma chants the names of the divine Mother
when the divine Father is praised in the West.
Mother and Father are two aspects of the same Reality.
Both are in each of us though most honor only one — but they should be integrated.
Fathers need to have motherly love and compassion or their discipline will become rigid
and repulsive; Mothers need to be able to discipline
as well as love and empathize with their children.
God, the One who loves and disciplines, does both in perfect balance.
The divine Father is the divine Mother and vice versa.

In India, the Supreme Being has for a long time been worshipped
not only in the masculine but also in the feminine form.

God is beyond the limitations of He or She
and should really be called It or That.
But if you must give God a gender,
She is preferable since She contains he.

The Mother is the embodiment of patience.
No matter how often her child blunders, she forgives and showers more affection.
Most mothers have this kind of love only for their own children
but the divine Mother loves all the beings in the universe
and guides them spiritually as well.

No matter how we picture God, it is universal Love that we experience.

Love, blessing, grace and compassion are synonymous for God.

A god who is angry is not God.

The essence of all religion is Love.

The way to worship God is to love and serve Life.

Religion contains the secret of Life—it teaches us to love, serve
and respond to Life with empathy and compassion.

God's Love is born in our hearts.

When we love, meditation and bliss happen spontaneously.

Every religion has two aspects: an outer intellectual shell—
the philosophical teachings elaborated in its scriptures—
and an inner spiritual core.

Religion is merely the outer skin.
Spirituality is the fruit.

Religion is a road sign that points the way to spiritual experience.

Religion points to the fruit of immortality.
But instead of picking the fruit, we tend to grab onto the pointer
and cling to the literal words of the scriptures
instead of the principles to which they refer.

Religious celebrations are designed to point us in the right direction.
Holidays, like Christmas, are a reminder to those who have forgotten
and a wake-up call to those who do not know the real meaning of life.

The ancient sages of India foresaw that the people of the coming age
would not be able to grasp the subtle Truth.
And so the idea of the temple dawned as a way of making Truth

accessible to people of grosser intellect.
Unfortunately the true function of the temple, which was meant to symbolize the body,
was seriously misunderstood and mystified.
The deity was intended to symbolize the soul in the sanctum sanctorum of the heart
and the temple to symbolize the seeker's multi-sheathed body
prostrating to pure Being.

Temples are sacred spaces where we feel the divine Presence more deeply.
But we must realize that the Divine is not limited to the sanctum.
God, the all-pervading Consciousness, enlivens everything that exists.
Only when we think and act with this knowledge
can we really experience God.

The heart is the temple where God should be enshrined.

The body and the mind are the instruments of spiritual practice
and our success depends on their condition.
We should take very good care of the body, which is the temple of Consciousness.

To walk the spiritual path we must feel Love for God—
not just for a person, an image or an idol—these are only the beginning.
Real Love for God means loving every aspect of Creation and seeing divinity in all.
The body is the temple of the Supreme Self.
When we are at the temple we should forget the building and remember
the inner dweller, the Knower—supreme Consciousness itself.

The body is the bridge to the inner Self—it is the temple of indwelling divinity.
Thus purification of the body is very important.

The purpose of Amma's temples is to offer a place where devotees can gather
and worship, hear spiritual talks, share food as a blessing, and discover opportunities
to help others—poor village children and neglected elders in need of education or care.
Most importantly, they are places where we can purify our minds.

Liberation requires grace—which only reaches us if we are pure within.

To become pure and receive grace we must serve others selflessly.
And to serve we need to maintain our bodies.

Every cell plays an important role in sustaining the body.
It is very beneficial for our physical, mental and spiritual health to imagine
the trillions of cells within us opening and radiating beautiful golden sparkling Light.
We should do this every day.

The purpose of Yoga is to increase our inner well-being.
Yoga is not limited to any one religion or faith.
It came to us from the ancient sages of India to help people reconnect to Nature
and reunite with pure Being.

India's great gift to the world is her culture of Self-realization—
the vision of human beings rising to the supreme peak of God-Consciousness.
Since ancient times an unbroken succession of God-realized souls
has incarnated in India to lead Truth-seekers to their goal.
Today modern society, disillusioned with the empty grandeur of materialism,
looks to the perennial philosophies of the East for guidance and refuge.

Religion points to God and the ultimate goal of spiritual realization.
To attain the goal we must go beyond the pointer.
If we become overly attached to the outer aspect of religion, we can easily be misled.

Humanity is greater than all religion and philosophy.
Religion, philosophy and politics are meant for humanity — not the reverse!

Religion should not be used to build walls between people but to build bridges
that connect those who are estranged.
It is essential to understand the deeper meaning of religion,
its true message of Love and compassion.

If we do not understand its deeper spiritual meaning,
religion is nothing but blind shackling faith.

The true target of religion is spirituality.
The arrows — those teachings we draw from the quiver of scripture —
should be chosen to awaken our spiritual nature.

Most religious preachers ignore the underlying principles and purpose of religion, focus on the superficial aspects, and are unmotivated to practice the teachings of their own faith.

Religion without spirituality is as lifeless as a bloodless limb.

The true power of religion is spirituality.

Just as we suck the sweet juice from the sugarcane and spit out the stalk, we should drink the spiritual essence and not keep hashing over externals. Too many people chew the stalk and spit out the juice.

Religions were not created to cause problems but to solve them. Once they become entangled with politics, they are like arrows that veered off course — and are very hard to correct.

Today the world of politics has become so corrupt
that it automatically weeds out the well-intentioned.
Anyone sincere is subjected to relentless, merciless mudslinging.

Many problems arise when religion is used as a tool to protect vested interests.
When spirituality is the goal, peace and unity prevail,
but when spirituality is not the goal, everything disintegrates.

The great Souls emphasized spiritual values
but their followers have emphasized institutions.
As a result, religions born to spread peace and unite people in a garland of Love
have spawned conflict and war instead.

The great Souls have been confined to small cages of religion
by ignorant people trapped in their inflated egos
who attack one another in the names of the great Souls.
As long as we continue to do this, religious understanding and collaboration
will be nothing more than a mirage.

Religion is a constraint constructed by human beings.
Like language, it is taught and eventually it conditions us.
As seedlings need a fence when young, we too need early conditioning.
But as the tree outgrows the fence, we should outgrow our religious conditioning
and become unconditional.

Absorbing true spirituality from religion
is as powerful as electricity generated from an atom.

Atomic energy can be used to create or destroy—the choice is ours.
Religion without spirituality is dangerous as an atomic bomb.

To say, "Only my religion is good and yours is bad"
is like saying, "My mother is virtuous and yours is a whore."

Those who say, "Only my religion is right"—are wrong.
Personal views about God are bound to be wrong.
God will only appear when all views disappear.

No authentic religious leader or saint ever said that Love and tolerance should only be offered to the followers of their own faith.
Spiritual values are universal.

Terrorism and violence in the name of any religion should be internationally condemned and strong action should be taken.

The willingness to listen to others, the ability to understand others and the open-mindedness to accept those we disagree with — are the signs of a true spiritual culture.

Many religious practices were designed for the needs of their times. In dealing with the problems of the Modern Age, we need to re-examine our practices and make the appropriate changes.

Religious leaders should stress the inner heart of religion and urge people to practice the core ideals—this will help us resolve conflicts.

We need to remember that religion is meant for humanity—
not humanity for religion!
Religion ought to help human beings become humane.

There are three things that make a human being humane:
A strong desire to know the deeper meaning of life,
the miraculous capacity to give Love,
and the ability to experience and give happiness.

Philosophies are fine, but can we actually live up to them?

People talk a lot, but actually do very little.
Talking and doing are two entirely different things.
Many people can go on and on endlessly about their high ideals
without connecting them to their own lives.
Such people are of no use to society.

A scholar holding forth on God,
who has not experienced God, is an absurdity.

God is experience.

The universal Self cannot be understood—only experienced.

We need to have a high ideal in our lives
and be prepared to sacrifice everything for it—
this is true spirituality.

Only when people of noble intentions put their religious ideals into practice
will their followers be filled with Spirit and inspired to act nobly.

Today we have a severe shortage of good role models.
Religious leaders should step forward and fill the vacuum,
highlighting the importance of Compassion through their example.

We do not need religious propaganda, but an earnest effort
to help people absorb the true meaning of their religion.

The essence of every religion is spirituality.
And the essence of spirituality is Love and Compassion.

To rise and awaken in Love is true spirituality.

There is love and then there is Love:
We love our family but not our neighbor's family;
we love our children but not other people's children;
we love our religion but not others' religions,
our country but not others' countries.
The transformation of limited love into unlimited Love
is the purpose of spirituality.

The importance of feeling and expressing Love and compassion for all
and the realization that everything is part of a greater Reality
is the essence of spirituality.

The fundamental principle of all religions is Love.

Spirituality — Love, peace and compassion — is the quintessence of all religion.

Christianity tells us to "Love your neighbor as yourself."
Hinduism says, "Pray for others to receive what you wish to receive."
Islam says, "Care for your enemy's sick donkey."
Judaism says, "Hating your neighbor is the same as hating yourself."
Each religion tells us to see and serve all as One
since one Being dwells in all things.

Diversity is the nature of Creation.
A true religious leader loves and worships every aspect of Creation, seeing in everything the manifestation of divine Consciousness.

It is important to respect the feelings and faith of people of all religious persuasions. Faith in the immense power of the inner Self will bring true unity among people and between Nature and humanity.

Our children should be taught the core values of religion as a part of their education.
The redeeming qualities of religions should be pointed out
and differences de-emphasized.
This is the only way to maintain mutual Love and respect in modern society
where religious diversity is a growing reality.

There is no harm in having many religions and faiths
but instead of thinking of them as different, we should focus on the unity
and the great ideals that all faiths teach.

To guide followers back to the true heart of religion,
leaders should condemn all forms of oppression and violence against women.

No authentic religion ever denigrates women!

Religious leaders should make an all-out effort to eliminate hunger and poverty,
encourage their followers to make service an integral part of their lives
and enlighten them about the grave importance of protecting our natural environment.

Divine qualities are the essence of every faith.
The principles of Love, compassion and unity are at the heart
of every true religious teaching.

Religions are floral arrangements for the worship of Supreme Being—
how beautiful it would be if they all stood together wafting the perfume of peace.

The Middle East gave birth to the three Abrahamic religions,
Judaism, Christianity and Islam.
Asia gave birth to Hinduism, Buddhism, Confucianism,
Sikhism, Jainism and Taoism.
These are considered to be the world's major religions.
Since most religious conflicts have originated in the Mid-East,
it is appropriate that religious conflict end there too.
If religious practitioners are prepared to think and act as a single unified force
unswayed by outsiders, unity and peace are possible—
no matter how impossible that may seem.

The universe is far too complex to be explained by any single religion or philosophy.
If we desire peace, contentment and progress, we should seriously try
to make the world understand the path of integral harmony,
the spirit of the eternal Way.

The true meaning of religion is faith in the existence of a supreme Power
and a life lived according to spiritual values and ideals.

Whatever our religion, if we remain steadfast in our faith
we will progress toward the ultimate goal.

Whatever our religion, if we understand its spiritual principles
we can reach the ultimate goal and realize our own divine nature.

Spirituality means awakening to our own true Self.
Those who make the effort to know the true Self are the truly faithful.

Spirituality is the key that opens the heart so we can view everyone with compassion.

We are meant to become someone who loves everyone.

If we can keep the flame of compassion burning within us we can banish the darkness around us.

Today, awareness of the importance of spirituality is growing. Our individual efforts to attain inner harmony are definitely benefitting the world.

In many ways people are now becoming more and more aware of the need for spiritual life.

May Amma's children shine like luminous flowers — like waves caressing the feet of God. May we see everything as supreme Consciousness and serve That selflessly.

May every trickle of compassion expand until it becomes torrential.
May every spark of Love become a blazing Sun that transforms Earth into heaven.
This capacity we have within us—as our birthright and our very nature.

May we say farewell to the dark age of rivalry and greet the dawn
of a new age of creative, inter-religious cooperation.
May the future generations call this the Millennium of Religious Friendship.

We have been deluded by the superficial aspects of religion, but we can correct this.
Together, let us realize that the real heart of religion is universal Love—
the pure-hearted perception of Oneness everywhere.

Never mind about religion—peace and Love are universal!

The people of any religion can rise to great heights
if we will let our hearts fill with Love.

10
WORLD PEACE

War is a bad habit.
It is not the way to bring peace.

War is not a solution.
In war so many innocent people are killed
and so much other damage is caused.
Amma says the attitude of hatred and revenge must be eliminated.
It will never solve our problems.

Violence is a reaction that does not bring about a solution—only more problems.
As long as there is life there will be problems—they are inescapable.
But we will never correct any situation by waging war.

Whether we do right or wrong, there will always be problems.
There is only one place on earth where there are no problems: the cemetery.

Good and evil will always exist in the world.

The world is a flower and every nation is a petal—
when one is diseased, the others are affected
and the beauty and vitality of the flower are at risk.
Is it not our responsibility to protect and preserve the lovely fragrant flower
of this world and stop its destruction?

Society is peaceful when we all perform our duties responsibly.
This means respecting one another and recognizing that we are all part of one Being.
We do not need the kind of peace that is forced, or that comes after death.

Compassion is the foundation of peace.

Compassion is the law and foundation of every society.

While language and culture vary from country to country,
peace and Love are universal.

Love is the only currency that is accepted in every country.

Amma has children all around the world with cultural differences
shaped by geography, economics and mental maturity,
but peace and Love are the same everywhere.

Language, class and color are never barriers to Love.
Love does not distinguish between religion, race, nationality or gender.
As a cow's milk is always white and fire is always hot and honey is always sweet,
Love is always Love — in every language, class and color!

Countless millennia have passed since the dawn of humanity.
We have been on a long journey in search of peace, prosperity and happiness.
We have made remarkable progress but now it is our duty
to make this millennium richer and more fulfilling than previous ages.
We should aim not only for a world thriving and prosperous materially,
but also for a world that is peaceful, cooperative, unified and compassionate.
To achieve this, we are going to have to evolve culturally, morally and spiritually.

How many wars has Man waged, how many children and innocents has he killed,
how many billions of dollars has he spent on wars and weaponry,
how many millions of people has he mired in fear, hunger and poverty?
And what has been gained by all this—who has benefitted?
Political and religious leaders, social workers and cultural ambassadors are constantly
talking about peace—but it is only a mirage.

There have been a few wars fought out of concern for human welfare
that achieved a greater good, but the vast majority were waged
to protect vested interests not to uphold truth or justice.
Their motivation was entirely selfish.

In modern warfare the enemy's country is destroyed in every possible way.
Victors plunder and monopolize land, resources and wealth for their greedy enjoyment.
Traditions handed down for generations are torn up by their roots
and innocent people massacred without mercy.

**Some wealthy countries even start wars simply to promote
the sale of their latest weapons!**

We cannot begin to measure the amount of toxicity
released by bombs and other weapons into our atmosphere and our soil.
How many generations have been forced to suffer physically and mentally, as a result?
Death, poverty, starvation and epidemics—this is war's gift to humanity.

No power-hungry, self-centered leader bent on protecting his own interests
has ever attained peace or happiness by conquering the world
and persecuting human beings.
His death and the days leading up to it were sheer hell—
history demonstrates this towering truth.

There is no end to the wars and deaths caused by Man
or to the tears shed by his tragic victims.
And what was it all for? — To conquer, establish his superiority
and satisfy his unquenchable appetite for wealth and fame.
Man has brought down upon himself curses beyond counting.
It will take more than a hundred generations to wipe up the tears,
console the suffering and relieve all the pain.
As atonement should we not at least try to reflect upon this and look within?

The world is going in a very strange direction.
We should be looking into ourselves and nowhere else.
We must look inside!

Today human beings are ruled by their desires and their anger.

In pursuit of worldly pleasures, we have abandoned the quest
for lasting spiritual happiness — turning our backs
on sweet pudding for crow droppings.

The minds of human beings are now almost like animals.

Man's ego is a horse with no reins.

People act like automobiles with no brakes—oblivious of their impact on others.

Today our mantra is speed.
Everything is falling apart, but no one slows down.

Fighting has become our primary response to life.
Love, compassion and kinship are rapidly vanishing.

There is enormous greed everywhere!
Our selfishness has grown so deep that people will resort to anything to satisfy their endless desires.

When we try to satisfy our unruly desires, we are always disappointed.
As soon as we satisfy one, another appears in its place.
We cannot distinguish between our real needs and our false needs,
and cannot reign in our desires for what is unnecessary.

Today people know how to take, but not how to give.

We view the world as an economy, not as a family.

Around the world we may have experienced an increase in wealth,
but with it has come a steep decline in ethics and morality.

The little we gain from our constant labor for a living—
what is that worth, really?

Contemporary society is full of people who, when given power and responsibility,
become arrogant and forget that they are merely human.

Everybody wants freedom and rights and no duties.
The more selfish and unrighteous we become,
the more we throw Nature off balance.

We all use one another—haves and have-nots is the way of the world.
Everyone exploits others.
Try to do something for the less fortunate—
a river is made of many drops.

Life is a blessing—not a right.

By fighting for our rights, we lose invaluable treasure
and cause irreparable harm.

The most serious problems facing the world today are mental pollution
and humanity's growing selfishness and cruelty.
These are the roots of all our other problems.

Everything is changing but our negativity.
Our personalities are a reflection of our minds.
The ability to rise to an occasion and act is dying out.
In the name of stability and competition,
we have become hateful, vengeful and stubborn.

Who are the enemies living inside us?
Ego, Hatred and Selfishness.
It is time to build an army to fight them—
an army of Humility, Service and Love for Being itself.
If we are willing to fight the battle of life with their assistance,
we will be able to find lasting peace and serenity.

To develop humility, service and Love,
we have to be able to control our thoughts, words and actions—
to be aware of the way we walk, sit and look at others.
We live in the past and the future—in our mad rush to fulfill our desires
we are not giving proper attention to our actions.

Right now a disaster is taking place — more destructive
than any world war, tsunami or volcanic eruption.
And either we are blind or indifferent to it.
That disaster is the fall of dharma, of human responsibility.

Humanity has almost reached the peak of *Adharma* — unrighteousness.

Today we think it is all right to do anything we want.
Customs and traditions considered "old-fashioned" have been discarded
in the name of "modernity".
Without them, we no longer know how to control ourselves.

Amma sometimes wonders if humanity is rousing its animal instincts deliberately
or simply helpless to prevent this from happening?
In any case, it is foolish to rely on human power alone — however great.
We shouldn't delay in connecting with our divine Power —
that is the strength we need!

Spiritual values are the cement that fortifies the structure of society
and without them, society falls apart.

If we do not remember that it is better to give than to take,
goodness, virtue and right conduct will perish from the Earth altogether.

Our society has four main weak points
that need to be corrected before it is too late:
Education without values,
sophistication without culture,
development without Nature and lifestyle without health.

Traditionally, the pursuit of dharma, or duty, wealth, enjoyment and liberation
were considered the four pillars of life.
Today society is like a four-wheel car with two flat tires.
Moral responsibility and the desire for liberation have collapsed
and only the pursuit of wealth and pleasure is functioning.
This is not enough—we need a truer vision!

If we do not restore dharma—our responsibility to life and all creatures—
all our efforts to achieve world peace will be in vain.

The whole world longs for peace and calm, but war and terrorism
keep spreading—so many innocent lives have been sacrificed!
To stop these meaningless killings we must take a deep look at the root causes.
Strict security checks are not a permanent solution.
There are explosives more dangerous than bombs and undetectable by any machine:
the anger, contempt and revenge hidden in the human mind.
Until they are eradicated, it is basically impossible to make the world peaceful.

Even if we put all the nuclear weapons in the world into a museum,
we would still not have world peace
because of all the weapons that remain in the human mind.

There is never a time when war is necessary—
but how can it ever be eliminated from the external world
when it is still being waged in our own minds?

Down through the ages, humanity has learned many lessons
from many experiences, but in many ways it has failed.
In the past century we endured two world wars that took the lives of millions.
Recently we have witnessed tragedies equally horrifying.
The threat of nuclear war remains
and the worldwide spread of terrorism is a grave concern.

Religious and ethnic persecution still plague humanity—
along with new problems of youth violence, drug abuse, child abuse and others.
Countless people die of senseless violence in our cities every day.
The problems of starvation, poverty, disease, environmental pollution
and extreme exploitation of Nature remain unsolved.

World history is primarily the story of hostility, hatred and revenge.
The rivers of blood spilled by Man, in his drive to possess and control
everything and everyone, have yet to run dry.
So cruel have been his actions that he seems to possess
not even a crumb of compassion.

If Man's destructive emotions are not eliminated,
there will be no end to war and violence.

Today we are witnessing the clash of past and future,
with the male community unwilling to compromise representing the past.

Until harmony has been restored between men and women—
between masculine and feminine—peace will be nothing more than a distant dream.

The much-discussed equality of men and women is not being practiced—
women are still being sidelined socially.
Expecting progress when women are marginalized is as foolish
as imagining we can fly with only one wing.

True humanity will dawn for women and men
only when masculine and feminine are in balance.

Women and men are equal in the eyes of God.

Which eye is more important—the left or the right?
Both are equally important.

Feelings of superiority and inferiority arise from the ego.
A man who feels superior to women has an inflated ego.
Inflation is a major weakness and very destructive.
A woman who feels inferior to men wishes to be superior—
which is another sign of the ego.
Both attitudes are wrong and unhealthy
and only serve to widen the gulf between the sexes.
If we do not bridge it with Love and respect, the future will grow even darker.

In the West, women cope with their oppression by acting like men—
thinking this will make them equal.

Amma has been happy to see that Indian women, while gaining the courage
of Western women, are preserving their maternal qualities —
for when we lose our hearts, we lose our culture too.

Women should not try to become equal by imitating men,
but should develop strong character, discrimination and determination
while maintaining their natural feminine gifts.

Many people believe that women should bear and raise children
while men should govern and command the nation — but this is wrong!
Women can govern as well as any man
when their latent masculine qualities are developed.

At no time in human history has a society with no respect for women
ever flourished — it has always collapsed.

Laws that block women's social progress and rightful freedoms
are not divine laws —
they are expressions of men's selfishness.

Real leadership is service born of Love and compassion, not domination and control.

What makes leaders truly courageous are compassion and friendliness.

What the world needs today are servants not leaders.
Everyone wants to be a leader but we should become servants instead.

To drive out the darkness and bring about peace,
we need the example of people who speak and act out of simple goodness.

Words spoken in sincerity can truly inspire and empower others.

Words have incredible power.

Everyone should become a role model
since there is always someone looking to us as an example.
It is our duty to consider those who look up to us.

We see in the world what we project.
If we look through the eyes of hatred and vengeance, the world looks horrible.
If we look through the eyes of Love and compassion,
we see divine beauty everywhere.

We see the world exactly as we are.

When we change, the whole world changes.

If we can change our mental perception, we can change outer things as well.

We cannot change the world in one stroke,
but the little that we contribute can make a great change.

Each kind word, each smiling face, each good action benefits our neighbor,
our community, our nation and our world.

Simply approaching issues with respect could create a major transformation
in society and the whole world.

The real change has to happen in each of us.
Only when our inner conflicts and traces of negativity are eliminated,
can we play a truly constructive role in establishing world peace.

To bring peace to the outer world, our inner worlds need to be peaceful.

To attain peace of mind, we need to reach equilibrium,
to bring the pendulum of life to a standstill
like the needle on a balanced scale.
For this to happen, we need meditation and other spiritual practices.

People will continue to suffer until we learn to balance material and spiritual life.

We can only be whole-heartedly non-violent and kind
when we shed our individual ego
and realize we are part of universal Consciousness.

Until then, let us try to love and serve others with that goal in mind.

**The human personality is a bundle of imperfections and limitations.
To really be able to benefit others
the personality must dissolve into divine Consciousness.
Only that Power, omnipotent and omnipresent, can save the world.**

**Because we have forgotten the true Self—which is blocked by our egos—
we experience the feeling of otherness.
Because we only know the small self, we are self-centered.
We need to outgrow this and center ourselves in the true Self—
which is absolute Being.**

**If we cannot transform the world, at least we can transform ourselves.
Society consists of individuals and every individual needs to be purified.
This is the only way we can change the character of the world.**

For the world to change, we need to change.
If we change, others will follow.

Waiting for others to change will not work.
Even if they do not change, we should be willing to change and do whatever we can.

Peace is much more than the absence of war and conflict.
Each individual, family and society must foster it.

We need to change our approach
and start thinking about how we can help others,
instead of how others can help us.
This is the way to peace.

Where there is Love, there is peace.
Where there is selfishness, there is always misery and sorrow.

True happiness and contentment come only from loving and serving.

It is not enough to love and respect our motherland —
we should love and respect all Creation, since there is nothing that is not divine.

God pervades everything — we should respect every single living being.

Love is our weapon.

It is time to end the cruelty and ruthlessness long enacted in the name of War.
War is the product of uncivilized minds.
The thought patterns involved must be abandoned.
Then we will behold the fresh green leaves and lovely flowers
and sweet tender fruits of Compassion.

In terrorists, criminals and warmongers there is no compassion —
Love has totally dried up.
May the prayers of millions of people create such an atmosphere of Love

and compassion that even their loveless minds are affected, however faintly.
Many innocent people suffer from their crimes.
Vengeance grows from within and even if only a few
harbor hatred, it can affect everyone.
Pray that they may learn respect and compassion and be pierced by Love.

The world does not need selfish loners
who only know how to threaten and destroy,
whose only language is the language of the ego,
who know nothing about Love and concern for others.
We need people whose hearts are full of compassion and Love.
They are society's strength and only they can bring transformation.

There are two kinds of ego:
The first is expressed through money and power;
the second, even more destructive, through the firm belief
that "my religion," "my point of view" is right and others' views are wrong,
unnecessary—in fact, intolerable!
Only when both are gone, will there be peace.

We must find every possible way to generate Love and compassion in everyone
and put it into practice — or the world will only go from bad to worse.
Amma hopes this will not happen.

In this deep forest of ignorance, ferocious animals surround us waiting to devour us.
A fire is approaching and our legs will not be strong enough to carry us away.
Pray to the Supreme, "I cannot save myself, please help me."
If you do, your heart will open like a stagnant pond opening into a stream
and the dam of separation will be broken.

With a compassionate heart, we can lead even the blind.

Gradually we can destroy our inner demon, the desire for War —
which is a giant curse on humanity and Nature —
and enter a peaceful and happy era.

We should gratefully accept the precious opportunity we are given
and advance on the road to peace and Love.

We should learn from history, but not live in it.

Scratching old wounds only irritates them more.

Let us not remain stuck in painful memories of past wars and conflicts
but forget our dark history of hatred and rivalry
and welcome in a new era of Love, faith and unity.
We must all work together for this.

If we want positive change in society, everyone must participate.
Everyone must be willing to make an effort and sacrifice.

If the source of war is in the mind of man, the source of peace is there too.
If we want to prevent future wars, we have to teach our children moral values.

Modern weapons can pinpoint targets with deadly accuracy.
If only our compassion reached the poor, the hungry
and the homeless with equal precision.

We may not be able to avoid natural calamities and, as long as we are ruled by the ego,
we may not be able to avoid war and conflict altogether,
but surely we can eliminate hunger and poverty, if we make a firm resolve.

Poverty is our great Enemy.
Poverty weakens the body and the mind
and causes burglary, prostitution, murder and terrorism.

Eighty percent of society's problems could be solved by eliminating poverty.

If the current generation could bring back a sense of duty and responsibility,
poverty and starvation would vanish like a bad dream.

The United Nations and all nations should establish projects to educate women
and eliminate female poverty altogether.

The United Nations should provide safe havens for women and children
in all regions of violent conflict.

All religions and nations should condemn the shameful practices
of femicide, female abortion, infanticide and genital mutilation.

The human mind is a mystery—a puzzle—
where truth and lies, gods and demons, good and bad are all mixed together.
One of the most deplorable, repulsive and dangerous afflictions of the human mind
is the drive to sexually abuse and exploit another human being.

We need to make a determined international effort to educate young males
with the aim of ending rape and violence against women entirely.

The frequency of rape around the world is truly shocking and the punishment of rape victims in some countries unbelievable! Can we simply stand by and watch this?

The United Nations and leaders of all nations should intensify their efforts to abolish trafficking in children and sexual exploitation of girls, and establish legal consequences truly prohibitive!

Governments should determine the best way to protect innocent young minds from sexually explicit material available on the Internet.

We should not tolerate assaults on the dignity of women by advertisements that portray women as sex objects.

Child labor should be abolished entirely, along with the dowry system.

Contemporary nations keep increasing their military power—
but Amma's approach is Love, patience and forgiveness.
The author of the epic Ramayana was once a thief, but the saints he tried to rob
were so patient that he eventually became a great saint.

Our youth are not good for nothing—they are good for everything.
They are not careless but uncared for.
The future of the world—the strength that can awaken society—lies in them.
If they wake up, the future of humanity is secure.
If they do not, the harmony of life and humanity will be severely disrupted.

Youth should be at the forefront of water, energy and forestry conservation campaigns.

Today, there are hundreds of nations and religions.
The very words often connote division and diversity
since each has its own characteristics, ideology and interests.
Diversity can be seen as a barrier to peace, prosperity and happiness—
but isn't it precisely what makes the world rich and beautiful?

Isn't the most beautiful bouquet the one with a variety of flowers?

**No one can deny the world's diversity, since that is its very nature.
When we reach a deeper understanding and embrace humanity's noblest values,
we will understand that the beauty of our world comes from this diversity.**

**May the many streams of human knowledge unite
to form a mighty river flowing around the world, overcoming national barriers,
bringing the waters of life and creating gardens of culture everywhere.**

**To adapt to another culture at the expense of our own is like cutting up our body
to fit into a dress, or eating an artificial apple to satisfy our hunger —
it violates and harms our natural way of being.**

**It is our responsibility to protect and nurture the beautiful flower of the world.
Nations should walk together sharing their best contributions
and adopting other countries' best practices.**

In a world of positive role models, weapons and war would not need to exist—
except as a bad dream in some distant past.
Arms and ammunitions would merely be artifacts in a museum,
symbols of a time when humanity strayed from the path to our true destination.

If world peace is to ever become a reality,
every human heart must fill with peace and harmony.
Love for humanity must reawaken in all of us.
Love and unity are not something alien, but fundamental human instincts
and the very foundation of our existence.

There is really no problem with the world—the problem is the human mind and ego.
Once the ego gets out of control, it creates many problems for the world.
More empathy and kindness would make a big difference.

If we ever want to end war and suffering,
we will have to learn to be compassionate, open to others
and truly understanding.

Amma often thinks that it would be so beautiful — like a child's game —
if bombs scattered chocolates, candies and heavenly fragrances instead of shrapnel,
or lit the sky with bright colorful rainbows.
If only the flashes of destruction were flashes of compassion!

When Amma looks back on the past year, She recalls so many tragedies —
lives and belongings destroyed by tsunamis, hurricanes, floods and terror.
And it seems that the whole world has fallen into the clutches of a large octopus of fear.

Let us all pray for world peace and imagine every heart on earth
filling with peace, Love, and joy.
Collective prayers are extremely powerful —
they can affect the future of humanity and the whole planet.
Pray for the victims, their families and also the offenders.

Let us grow and flourish as one family united in Love, celebrating and rejoicing
in our unity — in a world where peace and contentment prevail.

It is Amma's wish that her children dedicate their lives
to spreading peace and Love throughout the world.

Let us stand together and show the world that compassion,
Love and concern for all our relations have not disappeared from the Earth.
Let us build a new world of peace and harmony by staying deeply rooted
in the universal values that have nourished humanity since time immemorial.
Let us say goodbye to war and brutality forever—
reducing them to the stuff of fairytales.
May the future remember us as the generation of peace.

Only when human values become a part of the festival of life
will it be a true celebration.

Only through unwavering Love and faith in socially beneficial ideals
can we make and implement the right decisions.
Diplomatic promises and opinions change nothing.
To make a decision and implement it, requires thorough understanding
of our problems and must be followed by serious effort.

We should not continue to cater to the haves and push the have-nots into a deepening pit of expectation, despair and suicide with our empty promises.

A revolution is required now—not a worldly but a spiritual revolution!

Only the light of Love will ever banish the shadow of fear.

In hard times, we can either squander our strength by running away in fear or we can try to overcome our problems with Love.

During the past year we have witnessed many tragedies and troubles. Thousands lost their lives in wars and riots; many were victims of terrorist attacks; many died in natural calamities; and a great many lost their life's savings. The refugee crisis has reached a peak—countless minds are full of fear and despair. Nevertheless we should not drown in fright and dejection. The power to face such challenges is within us.

If all join hands, we can face the greatest of ills with serenity and optimism.

Loving your country means loving its inhabitants.
If you really love your country, love your people and serve them.
Do something to reduce their suffering.

We have been given a human birth to face and overcome challenges—
not to run away from them!
A ship in the harbor encounters no challenges
while a ship at sea has to weather gales and storms, whales and sharks.
But who would build a ship only to moor in the harbor?
When obstacles appear, we must rouse our inner strength, create an atmosphere
of selfless Love, and save those who are drowning in grief.

When difficulties arise we can either run away in fear
or kindle Love within us and try to conquer them.
When we run, we sap our strength and are scattered like leaves in the wind.
We cannot escape our own shadow, and if we try we soon collapse in exhaustion.

The shadow of fear vanishes only in the light of Love.
Love is our real strength and refuge.

The door to Love is always open—all we have to do is walk in.

If we can light the lamp of faith and Love in our hearts and move forward together,
we will banish darkness and create a real social transformation.

Though we may not be able to see in the light of a single dim bulb,
we can see when many bulbs are shining together.
Together we can accomplish so much.
Even the smallest action can have great significance.

One snowflake has little impact but when it melts into other flakes
a stream is born that joins other streams to eventually form
a mighty river coursing to the sea.

One drop does not make a river, but many drops create a flow.
From unity of Love, life streams forth.

The greatest journey in life begins with one step.
May we welcome the New Year with small changes in our lives.
If we all do this, it will mark the beginning of a new Age of Love and Compassion.

Together we are a power that cannot be overcome.
Working hand in hand with Love—not just the force of one life
but that of countless lives flowing harmoniously together—we cannot be stopped.

Let us say goodbye to the winter of selfishness and enmity
and welcome the springtime of Love, unity and peace.

There are many kinds of power in this world—
military power, intellectual power, word power.
With all these, we have tried and failed to bring about peace.
But the greatest power of all is Love.

Love is the power that can transform the world.

The problem of terror and bloodshed can only be solved by Love and compassion.

Anyone with weapons, money and expertise can wage a war,
but no one can defeat the power of Love—the knowledge that all are One.

Amma has complete faith in the transformational power of Love to unite all hearts.

May our faces be lit with smiles of Love.
May our minds be serene and fearless.
May our hearts overflow with compassion.
May the Sun of discernment illumine us with the determination
to create a peaceful and harmonious world.

Let us vow to change our approach to life.

Let us welcome the New Year by making small changes.
And if all of us do this, we will enter an entirely New Age.

When a new year dawns, it does not mean that the Sun has risen in the west.
Nothing changes simply because a number changes.
All we have is this present moment, so let us attempt to do something
to create a positive transformation.

Let us learn from last year's failures and enter this New Year
with more awareness, enthusiasm, optimism and faith.
Let us broaden the horizons of our knowledge and bless the year
with actions vibrant with kindness and Love.

Let us attempt to transcend feelings of anger toward those who have harmed us
and remember to express gratitude to our loved ones.
May we bring in a year that is a true rebirth—a new creation.

Let us resolve not to waste money on extravagances
when instead we can help sick children and truly bless their families.

The world needs to know that a life dedicated to selfless service is possible.

More than any economic or technological revolution,
an inner revolution that allows us to see others as ourselves
is the real need of the hour.
We must strive to love and serve all beings.

If we really want to, we can make a big difference in the world.
The benefit of our good and selfless actions will definitely come back to us.

May the tree of your life be rooted in the ground of Love.
May your good deeds be its leaves,
your kind words its flowers
and peace its fruit.

There are no barriers that cannot be overcome by Love.

Where there is Love, there is peace.

Pray for peace in the world.
Pray, pray, pray for the world.

Prayer is a sincere cry to the Creator that all may be peaceful and happy.

Imagine white flower petals falling from the entire sky all over the world—
on the mountains, the rivers, the oceans, the lands, the plants,
the trees, the animals, the people, and on your own head.
May the childlike innocence within you fill you with pure Love
as you chant *Lokah Samastah Sukhino Bhavantu*—
may all beings everywhere be peaceful and happy.

May grace protect us.

May God's grace guide and save us.

May the shadows of hatred and sorrow pass
and our minds fill with the golden light of Love and happiness.
May the dark clouds of poverty and conflict disappear
and the world awaken to a dawn of peace and prosperity.
May we be showered with supreme Grace.

May godliness awaken within us
and peace fall upon everyone everywhere.

11
OVERCOMING ANGER

**All our negative feelings like anger, hatred and jealousy
arise from the small self, the ego.**

**The source of anger is never external—it is always internal.
Anger is not caused by others, but by our own inner emotional wounds.**

**Many of us have deep inner wounds—there is so much pain!
Our wounds and pain give others the power to hurt us again and again.**

Anger is a deep wound festering in the heart that requires patient, tender, loving care.

Relaxation, not reaction, heals the wounds of the mind.

To react is to fight — fighting past trauma only deepens our wounds.

We must realize that the real problem is not what is happening externally but our reaction to it.

Reaction creates mental chaos and confusion —
merely thinking about reacting clouds our vision and discrimination.

Force and aggression are inherent in reaction.
The mind becomes turbulent and the disturbing thought we wish to forget rebounds with even greater force.

Reaction stirs up hatred, and hatred turns the mind into a living hell.

It is the mind that makes the world ugly or beautiful.

A situation is a problem only when wrongly interpreted.

We see good and bad in the world according to our mental tendencies.

The editorial mind cuts and pastes, manipulating what it hears to fit its requirements.

A negative thought is like a thief that can enter the mind at any moment and steal our most precious possession — our peace of mind.

Often, even if we can control others, we cannot control ourselves.
We speak and act in the heat of the moment and later on our words and actions come back to haunt us with even greater force.

Anger is like a blackout that makes us unaware of what we say and do —

and only afterwards do we realize our folly.

Physical wounds inflicted on the body are easily forgotten,
but inner wounds inflicted by angry words are very difficult to heal.

Do not get angry.
Anger will destroy your clarity of vision, your discrimination,
your self-control and your peace of mind.

Anger is very destructive.
Angry people are angry most of the time.
Even if their anger is not apparent, it is constantly boiling—
which makes it impossible for them to see and appreciate the good in others.
When someone does a good job, they do not congratulate them.
They cannot express love or be friendly.
Rigid and tense, they fly into a rage over nothing.

How can the flowers bloom in a boiling volcano of anger?

The ancient Indian god of speech is Fire.
A single word full of anger can cause great destruction.

**Like a jealous wife who finds the least excuse to be jealous,
an angry husband can also destroy his whole family and the lives of his children.**
Anyone who experiences their constant conflict and suspicion is poisoned.

Anger is not only toxic to the mind, but also to the body—
it over-stimulates all our cells, even our hair follicles.
When a snake gets angry, it releases its venom.
When we get angry, we poison ourselves and others.
In an experiment, an angry man's blood was injected into a guinea pig
and killed the pig within two minutes.

Anger, excitement and anxiety are all temporary states of madness.

The ways of the mind are very strange—
we miss many things that are right in front of our eyes.

Anger is like a computer virus that wipes out all the information.

Anger arises from the ego.
If we suppress it, it burns like coals in the mind,
makes us tense and disturbs both our words and actions.
But if we express it, we hurt others.
Anger is a double-edged sword without a handle—
it wounds both the wielder and the object.

When you harm another, you harm everyone—especially yourself.

Just as a stone thrown into a pond creates ripples,
anger spreads ripples in ever widening circles across society.
The widespread discontent and conflict we experience today is rooted in anger.

A single heart filled with anger and hatred can cause enormous damage.

Never let anger become a habit.

Negative emotions eventually produce harmful words and actions
until they finally destroy our mental peace altogether.
We need to become aware of our thoughts.

Whenever we have a negative reaction,
we need to contemplate the workings of our mind.

When we feel anger, we should neither express nor suppress it.
Allowing our anger to smolder is unhealthy.
We should try to calm our minds and contemplate the situation intelligently.
Most problems caused by anger can be avoided in this way.

We need discrimination to defeat our anger.

We should not act impulsively on any decision made in the heat of anger
or blurt out the words surging through the mind.
Discrimination and patience are the only effective antidotes.

Mindless speaking triggers the majority of today's problems.
Just as water crossing a boundary causes damage, words that go too far
can also cause widespread damage, and need boundaries.
Life should be enjoyed with kind words and actions.

Anger is overcome through patience.

Once our anger has subsided and we have reflected on the matter quietly,
we are able to see our own weakness.
We need to try to understand that anger is a childish weakness
and patience, true greatness.

Watching our thoughts as if gazing through a clear glass,
we can see the pettiness of our anger and the grandeur of forgiveness.

Some people experience happiness when they cause others unhappiness.
But when we are conscious of our thoughts,
we are not as easily provoked and manipulated.

When we explode in anger and create a scene,
we become sitting ducks for those who enjoy pushing our buttons.
Some people provoke anger as a pastime and make up stories just to upset others.

What we need is a cool head and a warm heart.
What we see in the world today is the very opposite —
most of us are hotheaded and cold-hearted.
Our heads are heated by worldly thoughts and our hearts are frosty with selfishness.
But if we can keep our heads cool, we can face the most adverse circumstances
and peacefully turn them to our advantage.

**Let us not become obsessed with what we think is right
but try to be considerate instead.**

The mental tendencies we have built up are like a pair of glasses
and each of us is wearing a different shade.

There are seven billion people on the planet and seven billion points of view.

All of us have our own ideas, which we think are right.
We have different opinions, thoughts and feelings
and believe that we are right and everyone else is wrong.
Everyone is like that!

Prejudice is an obstacle to a peaceful mind.
Gazing through the lens of prejudice, we cannot open our hearts and understand.
Only with an open mind can we accept and comfort others.

We expect too much of others — this is one of the biggest causes
of human suffering and disappointment.

People may love us to some extent, but expecting their Love only culminates in sorrow.

We must love one another since Love is the only thing that is real, but we should trust only God.

There is no point in wishing that fire gave light without heat. If we depend on someone, we may receive the light we seek for a while but should be prepared to get burned too, since our love is impure.

When you experience another's deficiencies, try to forgive them, not point them out.

If you fell into a hole, would you poke out your own eyes? Try to tolerate others' failings as you tolerate your own.

When you poke your eye with your finger, you do not punish it, you rub it, realizing that the finger and the eye are both parts of your own body.

Once we understand that others are part of our Self,
we will spontaneously feel compassion.

Just as we overlook our own mistakes, we should overlook the mistakes of others.

Christ set an unforgettable example for humanity when agonizing on the cross
He prayed for his enemies to be forgiven.

Forgive, forget and forbear.

Forgiveness is the way to peace.

To avoid suffering we need to understand the real nature of this world.

If we depend too much on outer things, we will be disappointed.
The world is forever chasing after material attractions —
but if we depend on such things, we are in for real disappointment.

Depending on the world is like trying to cross the ocean in a paper boat.

If not even the great Souls who were totally selfless
could make the world good through the power of their sacrifice,
what can we expect of powerless limited human beings ruled by selfish egos?
Instead of regarding others critically we should try to improve ourselves.

The desire for attention is inherent in human nature.
Everyone in the world—children, even animals—wants attention
and consciously or unconsciously seeks ways to get it—especially teenagers
who are dominated by the mind and the ego.

The ego cannot exist without attention.
As we grow up, the ego grows up too—it develops more subtle means
for attracting attention, but the craving remains.

The more egocentric we are, the more attention we feel we need.
We become hypersensitive and demand respect whether we deserve it or not.

An egotistical person is terrified of losing respect and importance,
and without it falls apart, becomes irritable and ill tempered.
An egotist cannot take criticism even if constructive
and needs to be the center of every moment.
Their whole life revolves around attracting attention.

Human beings, in general, try to attract as much attention as possible.
We want praise and recognition and consider it our right.
If we constantly feed our attention-seeking egos,
how can we ever know the true Self?

Instead of pointing the finger at someone else,
let us confront our own weaknesses—
this way most of our problems can be solved.
If we sincerely look in the mirror of our conscience,
it will not be hard to master them.

Let us stop searching for external causes, scapegoating others
and seriously try to overcome our own shortcomings.

Instead of dwelling on other people and things,
we should pay attention to ourselves and our own flaws.
Just as physical check-ups are needed to discover physical diseases,
inner check-ups, in the form of reflection on our spiritual condition, are also needed.
A disease diagnosed in a medical check-up can be treated.
Inner check-ups are equally important — they can help us
become more patient, better listeners, and so on.

It is very important to recognize our foibles and try to correct our behavior.

True strength comes from knowing yourself
and trying to overcome your own defects and limitations.

Continuous introspection is required to be able to see how we actually react.

Every night we should ask ourselves: "What good did I do today?
Did I hurt anyone? Did I get angry?
How can I avoid repeating the same mistake tomorrow?
How can I be kinder, more helpful, and make time for those in need?"
Doing this will fill your life with light and protect you from darkness.

The world's great spiritual masters have always taught us to respond, not merely react.
Their lives are living monuments to this great principle.

Try to see things as they really are.
The nature of any object or person cannot be different from what it is.
Understanding this allows us to respond properly and not overreact.

Do not try to turn a frog into an elephant or an elephant into a frog.
Try to see others for what they are, not what you wish them to be.

With anger we cannot change another's nature—only Love can do that.
Understand others and pray with Love and sympathy for their well being.
Try to be kind when others upset you.
This is a true response and will calm the mind.

Praying for others without feeling compassion
is like pouring fresh milk into a dirty cup.

Be angry, if you wish, about a worker's laziness
but do not be angry with the worker himself.
His or her humanity and Consciousness is the same as yours
and deserves your respect.

Try to respect people who insult you and understand that they do you a favor
by teaching you to learn patience and stillness.
Allow yourself to feel pity, concern and compassion for their painful past.

Every person has hidden trauma and misery.
We should be careful about judging others.

Laugh heartily whenever someone insults you.
Take their words as an expression of their traumatic past.
Try not to respond in kind and eventually not to feel any negativity at all.
Act but do not react, and you will enter a deeper state of consciousness.

Even when you are seething inside, try to realize that your accuser is suffering
and it would be cruel to hurt someone in such pain.
As a seeker your aim is to be compassionate and kind.

Be generous, try not to speak harshly
and eventually to harbor no ill feelings at all.

If you feel pity, concern and compassion, you will be able to forgive.
Imagine that Mother is speaking through them and quietly move away.

If you cannot leave, think of beautiful memories or inspiring ideas
that can help you maintain your silence.

We should avoid all situations that inflame our negativities and pollute our minds.

Letting a negative person influence us is like dumping ashes on our spiritual life.
We should not allow others to bury us in the ashes of their negativity.

Leave an abusive atmosphere when you must.

We should try to avoid situations that stimulate our negative habits.
Every time we get angry, we intensify the tendency, create more work for ourselves and prolong the journey to Self-realization.

Praying for those who offend us helps the mind to stay calm and peaceful.

Try to feel compassion for those who offend you—
try to empathize with those in pain.

If you cannot love, at least do not get angry.

A person who cannot control his or her anger
is as disabled as someone who is physically disabled.
We should be as sympathetic as we would be if they had a physical disability.

Invoke inspiring thoughts and good memories to help your mind stay calm.
Meditate, pray, chant or contemplate to eliminate your disturbing emotions.
Once you can feel compassion, you will be able to forgive and forget.

Forgiveness without a trace of hatred or revenge is a true response.

Children, *ahimsa*, the principle of non-injury, should be our life vow.
Ahimsa means refraining from causing pain to anyone
through thought, word or deed.

In the face of anger, be patient.

Before reacting to a situation pause and contemplate it.

If someone gets mad at you, instead of reacting simply ask yourself,
how can I feel anger when we are all the Supreme Self
with the same Consciousness?

We misunderstand and make mistakes because we do not realize who we really are.
How can anyone who really understands that the *I* in me is the *I* in you
ever become jealous or angry with someone else?

Hindu scriptures say that the same divinity exists in all beings,
whether human, dog, cat, cow, bird or plant.
How can there be any place for anger or hatred when we see divinity
enthroned everywhere?

**To maximize happiness and minimize sorrow,
we need to see everything as divine—as an extension of our true Self.
Whenever someone makes a mistake,
we should try to forgive them and see them as another us.**

**When we poke our eye with our finger, the same finger soothes the eye
because we know that both are part of us—of one Self.
We need to awaken to that state of Oneness.
Another's sorrow is our sorrow, another's joy is ours too.**

**Everything is one Consciousness.
We need to be able to see everything as inseparable from ourselves.**

Be considerate to everyone since everyone is a doorway to your Self.

**If you feel anger toward someone, speak to them, smile at them
and eventually your anger will pass.**

If you imagine that everyone is sent to you by God or Mother,
you will be able to be kind and loving to everyone.

Imagination is extremely powerful.

When the Sun shines on a thousand pots of water, a thousand suns shine in them.
When we understand what we really are,
we will see the Supreme Self reflected in everything.
Be kind, overlook others' imperfections and let Love dawn within you.

Constantly contemplate: Happiness is internal, not external.
In every action see God.

The smile that blossoms on our lips is God's signature on our face.
Never let sorrow or anger erase it.

See the Supreme Self in everyone.

Love and serve all.

12
GOOD QUALITIES

Children, God has given us the ability to become godlike.

Within us, immense knowledge is waiting to unfold.
But it can only do so with our permission.

Throughout history, the great Souls have been showing us the way—
patiently trying to teach us again and again.
But the choice to go on the journey is ours.

It is easy to wake up someone who is sleeping,
but very hard to wake up someone who is pretending to be asleep.
Most of us would rather keep our eyes closed to the truth.

Today we breathe, move and live in ignorance—in an almost totally unconscious state.
Even when we appear to be awake, we are dozing.

Inattentive, indiscriminant and uncomprehending,
we scarcely know what we say when we speak.
No wonder we find it difficult to enjoy each other's company.

We are too impatient to pay attention to the words we say and the things we do.

We expect others to be patient with us, even though we are impatient with them.

Everything has an inner as well as an outer form—but we are no longer aware of this.
We are like clothes worn by no one.

We are insincere, untrusting and unloving.
Our words drip with bitterness.
We have exchanged fresh and spacious playgrounds for grimy cell phones.

Love, beauty and all the divine qualities exist within us
but they are only realized by practice.

To become a good person, whose words and actions emanate goodness,
takes continuous effort.
We need to recognize our errors,
regret them and keep trying to eliminate them.
This is dharma, our human duty.

Instead, we try to find the easy way out by focusing on others' mistakes,
boasting about our own accomplishments, and blaming others for our failures.

We have the capacity to become whatever we choose.
We can choose to become a soul that wants only the good of others

and expresses this in its thoughts and actions,
or we can choose to become the epitome of evil.

Human beings have been given the freedom
to write whatever we wish on the pages of Life.
The pen and paper are provided, but we are not told what to write.
Hints are given regarding the consequences, but it remains for us to decide
whether we will write words of evil, hatred and ugliness
or goodness, Love and beauty.

Freedom of choice is the supreme blessing of human existence.
To fulfill the potential of this blessing, we must have the faith and innocence of a child.

Children are the most receptive of people.
They have faith and do not doubt—they do not resist life or love.

To gain spiritual knowledge, we need the mind of a beginner.

To gather knowledge, we need to bend.

The attitude of a beginner — innocent openness and receptivity — is always needed.

We have to be as innocent and humble as a baby.

Only with humility can new knowledge be gleaned.

To learn, we need a childlike mind that is not too proud to obey.

To learn to play the flute, even a Nobel Laureate needs beginners' training from an experienced flutist.

It takes an innocent, receptive beginner's mind to be truly creative.
Only with such a mind can we learn — and then it is easy.

The three essential qualities of a beginner are attention, patience and enthusiasm.

If we are eager and innocent, it is not difficult to understand the truth.
As lightning illumines a road in the darkness, innocence shows us the way.

We should take every situation in life as an opportunity to learn.
Every experience in life has something to teach us.

Time is said to be a great teacher, but Experience is the greatest Teacher of all.

Life teaches us many lessons, and presents us with many tests.
Our positive experiences become a source of inspiration.
And our negative experiences are an opportunity to correct our mistakes and grow.

Lessons can be learned from everything when we are awake and aware.

A mirror can either be used to clean your face or look into your heart.
It is very important to learn to see yourself clearly.

Instead of viewing others' flaws under a magnifying glass,
we should examine our own.
Eliminating hatred and indifference begins at home.
When our minds are bright and clear,
the world becomes bright and clear too.

We should accept every sentient and insentient being as our teacher.

Consider everyone to be a messenger from the Supreme.

Pay close attention to the virtues that others possess and you yourself lack.

Try to recognize and appreciate the good in others.

Seeing the good reduces our own suffering.

Like a swan extracting milk from a mixture of milk and water,
try to extract the good from everything.

Search for the goodness in others as meticulously as you would
if you were searching for a diamond in feces.

Drink the divine Essence and discard the rest.

Like the honeybee, gather nectar wherever you go.

See everything as God.

Painful experiences, when understood deeply, are beneficial.

From pain comes the message *It is time to change.*

To reach the state of joy we must first experience pain.
Pain is an unavoidable part of life.
Without suffering, we cannot truly appreciate either peace or happiness.

Suffering is a blessing that helps us to reach God.

The problems that we encounter in life make us stronger.
God creates them in order to strengthen us.

Suffering is inevitable whether we attain our desire or not.

The attitude that we will accept nothing less than success is wrong.
We must be able to accept defeat as well.

Sins can be washed away by tears of genuine remorse and repentance.
Through them we can escape the consequences of our mistakes, no matter how grave!

There is no sin that cannot be washed away by repentance—
as long as one is not like an elephant bathing in the river only to roll again in the mud.

The realization that we have done something wrong is liberating—
we are automatically forgiven.
The remorse that we suffer is our cleansing.

The eternal Way teaches us that everything is divine and no hell lasts forever.
No matter how great the wrong, we can still purify ourselves
with good thoughts and deeds, realize our divinity and attain supreme Consciousness.

Do not carry unnecessary burdens in your mind—
release them and be at peace.

Life is a blend of success and failure.
Strive to accept both with equanimity, composure and calm.

Equanimity is the ability to face different situations with the same tranquil attitude.

Once we can see that life and all it brings is an extremely precious gift,
we can say Yes and accept everything.

We should not be disheartened by our failures — victory is always on the way.
Remember this and move on.
Or take failure as the result of your past actions — or as God's will.
Otherwise your life will be very unhappy
and if you become disheartened, you will not succeed.

Any effort or attainment can be engulfed by the waves of life,
but do not feel disheartened and turn back!
Face the challenges with courage and keep going.
Then your life will be of benefit to others and you will find contentment.

Failure is a natural part of life.
Let us accept it as a necessary process of learning, and carry on.

The value of one's life is not determined by the number of successes or failures
we experience, but by what we do with them.

Setbacks do not make us a failure—only loss of confidence can do that.

Self-deprecating thoughts are not good for a seeker or anyone else.
We are blessed with the precious gift of human life.
With this body, mind and intellect we can learn to do what we wish.

If we fall down we should think, "I fell in order to get up"—
not "It is quite comfortable down here."
We should never feel shattered but always try to stand up and go on.

Both good and bad experiences are the way of the world.
We should learn to convert challenges into stepping-stones to success.
To do this we need a discerning mind that operates on spiritual principles.
Let us be happy and content with whatever comes our way.

Let us not spend our lives regretting our losses.

Circumstances are not changed by sorrow and lament—so why indulge in them?
A wound needs more than tears—it needs a healing balm.
In a crisis, we should look for a remedy immediately.

After numerous trials and tribulations comes the eternal peace of Love.
To reach the highest Bliss, a process of purification is necessary.
As impurities burn away there is pain and sacrifice.

To realize the Soul, the mind must dissolve.
After the loss comes the profit.

Spiritual realization is impossible without undergoing suffering.
We are imperfect at birth and progress through action.
A river has to flow many, many miles to reach the ocean.

Suffering is the bridge to God.

Suffering is the great Guru.

Let us forgive and forget our failures and our resentments
and allow warm memories of Love, friendship and joy to lift our spirits.
Life is nothing but a remembering and a forgetting.
Once we release the past, we can meet life with fresh enthusiasm.

Life is a garden — flowers, leaves and branches all naturally wither,
drop and become compost for the leaves and flowers to come.
Let us turn our mistakes and painful moments into compost for our growth
and welcome life with renewed vitality, ardor and joy.

When the old dead parts drop, the lovely new flowers will appear.
Let us clear away our old hurts and grievances, forgive and forget what we can,
and embrace the fresh new life that is budding.

It is pointless to worry about past mistakes—let us try instead to shape the future.
Cows never return to the same field to graze—only human beings
waste precious time ruminating over the past.
But we can change this harmful habit with practice.

Do not hurt anyone with your thoughts, your words or your deeds.
Listen to your conscience and follow it!

When we harm anyone, we harm everyone—especially ourselves.

Words are incredibly powerful and must be used with immense care.

Every word has the power to inspire as well as to destroy.

A single negative thought can destroy the whole world.

Every thought, word and deed has consequences.
Both good and bad actions affect many others.

Every thought and action has the power to brighten or darken many lives.

Thoughts — like viruses — are contagious.

Regardless of whether we realize it or not, our actions influence others.
We should always set a good example, for there is always someone
looking to us for inspiration.

Our words should be consoling.
We were given tongues to console, not to ridicule and cause pain.
Our actions should always be noble.

A positive action will bring greater happiness.

All our actions reverberate throughout Creation.
Our good actions are insurance coverage for hard times—
when they will return to us in the form of good karma.

Words that hurt others come back to us as bad karma.

Karma is simply our actions returning to us as our future fate.

The action we perform in the present determines
whether we experience good or bad in the future.

We have to reap the fruits of our actions—this is the law of Karma.

When we look in the mirror and smile, the mirror smiles back.

Remember, everything you do in life comes back.

Karma is like a boomerang that comes back and hits us if we do not catch it—
though unlike a boomerang, it may not hit us immediately.

Karma is the way we pay our debts.

There are three types of karma: the kind that can be eliminated,
the kind that can be reduced
and the kind that must be lived out.

The first type of karma is like a dusty mirror we can dust off.
The second is like coals we can revive with remedial actions.
The third is like a chronic stomach ulcer we must endure—all we can do is pray.

We are the cause of all that we experience.
We are the source of it all.

Cycling from birth to birth, we create our own karma.

Suffering is not accidental but the result of our past actions.
Here, the word *past* includes not only the past in this life and body
but in all our past lives, forms and names.

There are certain circumstances we cannot escape —
in that case we should be courageous and face up to them.

Our karma will come for us wherever we are and all we can do is pray.

The cycle of karma is as mysterious as God Itself.
Karma has no beginning but it does have an ending —
it ends when the ego ends and we have fully realized the true Self.

The power of karma veils the true Self.
At the same time it creates the urge to realize the Truth and return to the Self.
The cycle of karma, properly understood, is a great transformer.
Its powerful message is that our lives result from our past actions
and our present actions determine our future.

Beware! Both good and bad actions are rewarded accordingly.

The circle of karma will continue until we stop reacting
to the present, which was caused by the past.
When we accept experience as an inevitable consequence of our actions
and face it without anger or revenge, the cycle will finally stop.

The way to stop the law of karma from operating is to live moment by moment in God.
Once we realize the true Self, we will learn all about karma—
the mysteries of our previous births will be revealed
and we will know the secrets of the universe and all Creation.
There is no other way to understand the Mystery.

The law of karma is very subtle.
To understand it is to understand God.

To a true spiritual seeker, the ultimate message of karma is:
Break the cycle, close the account, and be free.

Once we attain perfection, we will know that the real Self
always has been and always will be.
It was never born and will never die — It is beyond the law of karma.

We cannot foresee the future or even what tomorrow will bring.
Be very careful in your actions today,
for we cannot know what their repercussions may be.

The law of karma is a matter of faith and cannot factually or logically be proven.
Descriptions and explanations of karma are meant to prevent people

from harming themselves and others, and drifting ever further
from their divine nature.

We need to exercise the greatest patience with our subordinates
or their heart-rending prayers may return as a curse upon us.
The cries of helpless anguished hearts have great power.
Waves of pain rush in and flood our aura,
which changes according to the effects of our actions.
When we do evil that hurts another, our aura darkens.
Our inner light becomes invisible and divine grace cannot reach us.

We should keep remembering God during every action we perform.
God is the life force in all the beings in this universe.
The kindness we show each life will return as God's grace.
To be blessed with grace, fill every look, word and action with kindness.

Be very careful with your words and your glances —
our eyes can say even more than our words.

Our good actions will eventually return as God's grace.

When we identify with the mind and the body as "I"
and believe that "I am the doer," we cannot receive God's grace.

We should perform our actions responsibly
but without considering ourselves the doer, for all power flows from God.

It is God's strength flowing through us that we experience as our own
whenever we act and accomplish something.
Remember the source of the Power that makes all action possible
and never presume to be the owner.
Our strength comes from the Supreme Being.

Focus on your actions not their results, or the ego will interfere!

The strength to act comes from the Whole.

A higher Power shines in us as beauty, truth and goodness.
When our lives radiate that Power is when we are truly strong.

Employ the body meaningfully to seek and find the Soul—
this is the true meaning and purpose of life.

These bodies that we are blessed with are intended for doing good.

The body is meant to act for God, not only for its own pleasure.

Worldly life depends entirely on the sense organs,
but if we overly indulge them, we drain away all our energy.

Vegetarians are calmer and more *sattvic* like herbivorous deer;
meat-eaters are rougher and more *tamasic* like carnivorous tigers.

To reach liberation we need grace, which can only reach those who are pure.
To become pure and earn grace we need to serve the world unselfishly.
And for that, we need a healthy body.

Hospitals and medical treatments are certainly not in conflict with spirituality.
They help us sustain the body—the instrument for knowing the Self.

Let us work with Love while we are still healthy.

We may not be blessed with monetary wealth, but if we have a healthy body
we can enjoy our work and avoid burdening others.

Life is a precious gift and the human body is a rare boon.
Let us not idle away our lives.

Children, do your work sincerely,
whether you consider it important, enjoyable or not.
Always show interest and Love as you work.
When Love enters into it, work becomes easier and soon effortless.
When Love blossoms, it blossoms in all our actions.

Let your work be your spiritual practice.

No work is insignificant or meaningless.
How significant and beautiful our work is, is determined
by the amount of Love and attention we put into it.

In any field — spirituality, science, politics or the arts —
our success depends upon the depth of our sincerity and dedication.
All actions performed with loving care and attention bring us closer to God.

Play when you play, study when you study, and pray when you pray!

How we do something is more important than what we do.

Pray for God to illuminate everything you do.

Through good thoughts and works let us turn our precious human lives into a perpetual act of worship.

In every action worship is the right attitude.

Worship and devotion do not run from duty and responsibility or act without Love and compassion.

Adopt an attitude of surrender and selfless service.
Only when we surrender our ego, does action become worship.

With the right attitude every action becomes worship.

Everything depends upon our mental attitude.

Let us see every action as worship of God.

Let us perform all our actions as well as we can,
using all the strength given to us,
and then let life unfold according to the supreme plan.

Life is a great mystery we can only understand by surrendering to it.
The intellect can never grasp life's grandeur, infinite nature or ultimate meaning.
Only when we humbly bow to life, can we know its true meaning.

Our humility is crucial.

Humility makes surrender possible.

If we can surrender and keep making an effort, we will finally attract divine grace.

When the head and the heart act as one, grace bestows fulfillment.

We can only control things to a limited degree—beyond that, everything happens by divine grace.
In the end, all our efforts must be surrendered.
Even the winner has to bow her head to receive the gold medal.

Only if we become a zero, can we be a hero.

Grace naturally flows into work that is performed with humility.
Thanks to humility, our work becomes a joy.

Be willing to bow to any and every thing.

It is only through humility that we can rise.
Within every seed, a tree lies dormant.
But if the seed remains in the storeroom, it will be eaten by the mice.
Only by yielding to the ground, can the seed mature into a tree.

The button has to be pressed down for the umbrella to open up
and provide us with protection from the pouring rain.

Humility is a requirement for grace—
not obsequious groveling but the humility of pure Love.

Humility is the key to the heart.

When we are humble we are not judgmental—
we are receptive and willing to go deeper and learn more.

Only the realization that we know nothing will help us to develop internally.
Those who understand this are the truly wise.

Humility, not acclaim, is the indication of true greatness.

Humility and patience are the very foundation of life—
but today there is conflict everywhere.
The world has become a battlefield.
Families, friends and lovers behave like enemies who aim to destroy.
First we gang up against outsiders, then turn upon each other.
Arrogant—willfully selfish—we have become capable of anything.

Children, try to cultivate patience. Love and trust.

If we row a boat that is tied to the dock, we will never cross the river.
We must release the thought of *I* and see ourselves as a pen or a brush in God's hand.

Everything that happens is part of the divine plan—
which is far wiser than the human plan.

Modern man prides himself on his abilities, yet is struck dumb by life's challenges.
In every human heart a battle rages between good and evil,
positive and negative, selflessness and selfishness.
Those who choose the path of righteousness are the blessed.

When we surrender our egos and empty our hearts, divine grace automatically enters.
But when we identify with the mind and body
and see ourselves as the actor or doer, grace cannot penetrate.

Imagine an egocentric well thinking, "The village gets all its drinking, cooking
and bathing water from me, and without me could not exist"—
ignorant of the spring that is its Source.

Our real center is God.

We go round and round in circles on the surface of life
in our incessant search for happiness, until we discover the Center within us.

Surrender opens the path to the Self.
An infinite power Source is within us, but only by surrendering
can we connect to it.

We must surrender to the Supreme Being.

Nothing happens by our own will—neither the next moment
nor the next breath is under our control.
We should surrender our work and doership to the Almighty—
realizing that only God makes any work possible at all.
Every act should be an act of worship.

May we cultivate an attitude of surrender.

To obtain grace, the finite sense of self must be surrendered.
We must stay alert and make sure that our motivations are pure—
and this takes real effort!

A lazy man, who makes no effort to attain grace for his soul,
receives none even when it showers upon him.

When we write with a pencil, we can erase our mistakes.
But if we keep making and erasing our mistakes, eventually the paper will tear.
Children, try not to repeat your mistakes.
It is natural to make mistakes but try to be more careful and attentive.
Only actions performed with keen awareness will take us to the goal.

External carelessness leads to internal carelessness.

Alone even in a crowd, distant from our true nature,
a stranger to our real Self, we rely on other people's reactions.
Try to overcome your limitations and do not worry about what others think.

Remember your true Self in every action you perform.

For spiritual aspirants all work — every look, word and action —
should be a spiritual practice.

It takes constant awareness and effort to say kind words,
do kind works, and be patient and compassionate.

Transformation takes great effort.

Perseverance is a necessity for self-improvement.

Patience and urgency must go hand in hand.

Continuous practice is the only way to ultimate success.

Repeated good actions will slowly become good habits
until finally our good habits become spontaneous.

Patience is a powerful mantra.

Patience is the goodness within us.

Patience has enormous power to awaken the goodness within us as well as others.

If we cultivate one divine quality, others will naturally follow,
and we will become an example for others and eventually transcend everything.

If we take one step toward God, God will take a hundred steps toward us.

The light of goodness shining in our hearts will annihilate our selfishness.

When we practice attentive awareness in our actions, we will forget ourselves.
The mind will become single-pointed and we will be happy.

When we eliminate all our weaknesses, negativities and limitations
God will be born in us.
We will be reborn and the old will become new.

Once we can see God's presence in others, we will have the humility
needed to overcome the ego and our life will become an offering.

Look closely, dear children, and you will see that all of life is a sacrifice.

Every celebration is preceded by a period of sacrifice and austerity.

Every life is a story of sacrifice—only through sacrifice does the world exist!

Behind every great and memorable event there is always a human heart.
Behind every good cause is a person who renounced everything and gave his or her life.

Love and selflessness are the source of all truly great achievements.

As spiritual people we should try to lead a life of pure and simple self-sacrifice.

Allow the goodness within you to blossom fully.
Save room in your heart for others.

Live for others, not only for yourself.

The purpose of every action is to serve.

Every action should be of service.

As we help those in need, selfishness will fade away
and suddenly without expecting it, we will experience fulfillment.

Devotion and knowledge are the two sides of the coin of spirituality
and service is the seal.

It is not what we receive but what we give, that determines the value of our lives.

If we are willing to take less and give more, we can begin
to unwind the ropes of our karmic destiny.

It is only what we give that we can ever hope to receive.

Instead of thinking, "What can I take?"—ask, "What can I give?"

One day the body will die, so why not wear it out in service before it rusts?

The seeds we keep to ourselves cannot sprout or bear fruit.
Only when we plant them in the earth will they grow into fruitful trees.
Only the talents we share will flourish.

A spiritual person should be like a tree that gives shade even when it is being felled.

What makes a tree so beautiful is its readiness to share everything.
Let us be inspired by it and never forget its example.

Let us be candles that illumine the world, even as we melt.

Do not live for yourself alone.
We are interdependent—the condition of the world
is a collective responsibility.
All of us must participate in its improvement.

Society consists of individuals whose thoughts and actions influence its culture—
a positive change in one person affects others.

In many ways people are becoming increasingly aware
of the need for a spiritual life.

Today, awareness of the importance of spiritual principles is spreading
and the efforts of so many people to attain inner harmony
are definitely benefitting the world.

The main obstacle on the road to happiness is our thoughts.
Unable to forget ourselves and be compassionate,
we crave achievement and acquisition.
Without conquering the ego, we cannot experience life's bliss.

The main hurdle to our happiness is the ego—our thoughts about ourselves,
our inability to forget ourselves and remember others,
our constant preoccupation with what to get and how to get it.

Ambition and desire arise from the ego's relentless,
crafty, impassioned claim for attention.
Amma is not suggesting that we should have no ambition
but that we should not be self-centered, arrogant and enslaved to our desires.

We ourselves create the ego by thinking of ourselves as separate.

As long as the ego remains, anger will remain.

Contentment comes from egolessness and egolessness comes from Love,
devotion and total surrender to God.

We can write volumes about spirituality,
compose beautiful poetry, sing lovely songs, and talk about it
in the most flowery language, but until we actually experience it within us,
we will never really know its beauty and bliss.

May the supreme Consciousness take charge and remove all of our obstacles.
May we allow the river of all-embracing Love to run its course.

If we can renounce I-ness and become empty, divine grace will fill our hearts.

When we overcome the small sense of I, we will become an offering to the world.

May we constantly cultivate and strive to maintain the attitude
that we are instruments of God—only then will grace come.

Grace is the outcome of actions performed in humility.
Humility is what makes our actions sweet.
When we act with heart and intellect together, grace will descend
and our lives will become complete.
Humility is essential.

Children, bow to everything,
determined to see the same Consciousness everywhere.

Always remember the Supreme.

Bow to the divinity of Earth and Sky.

When handling a hand-made object, think of the one who made it.

When talking to a friend, imagine the Beloved.

Perform all your actions with devotion.
When you rise in the morning, bow to Mother Earth.
Bow to your parents, your elders and teachers, and ask for their blessing.
When you take up a book or a pen for study, bow to it.
When visitors come, stand and offer them a seat and nourishment.
Never fight or strike anyone.
These are the basic rules of devotion to the Spirit.

The ability to see only good everywhere must become second nature.

This is true spiritual progress.

Real spiritual growth is reflected in the qualities of equanimity,
the strength to be patient, and the capacity to see goodness in everyone.

Every time a situation arises which makes us feel like cursing God or someone else,
let us remember that there is a positive side and that we must learn to see it.

Just as food and sleep are essential for the body,
a healthy diet of positive thoughts is essential for the mind.

Thinking a positive thought is like walking into a perfume factory.
Thinking a negative thought is like descending into a coal mine.

In essence we are pure, but as long as we keep filling ourselves
with negative thoughts, it is very hard to change.

Negative thoughts can only be eliminated by filling the mind with positive thoughts—
until finally there is no room left for the negative.

Real freedom is only possible when all our negativity has been uprooted.

We should become aware of our negative tendencies and try to weaken them—
not by fighting them, but by thinking good thoughts.

If we carefully install the precious gem of divine Thought in our hearts,
we will be able to cross to our destination.

In time, our good thoughts will completely dissolve all our bad habits.

As we improve, our patterns of action and reaction will relax.
And as our hearts begin to open,
we will open to the positive qualities of forgiveness, tolerance and harmony.

Once we change our attitude we will be able to see
the goodness that abounds in the world.

To recognize and realize the beauty and grandeur of the goodness of life,
it is necessary to experience the evil as well.
Otherwise, how would we ever know goodness —
with nothing to compare it to?

May we learn to see everything as the supreme Soul and feel no revulsion for anything.
May our minds flow in the all-pervading presence of the supreme Being.

God is nothing but goodness and God resides in everything.
To see God, all we need is a heart.

Scientists say that "Everything is energy."
The sages say that "Everything is the supreme Reality."
With the right perspective on life, we can see goodness everywhere.
Goodness dwells in our hearts and when we feel it, we feel happy.

When we lovingly recognize the goodness of others, our own goodness comes to life.
Looking back, we realize how much we owe to countless beings—a debt
it would take lifetimes to repay, particularly to Nature and ultimately supreme Being.

The positive goodness that awakens in us when we feel thankful
blesses all of humanity and the entire world.

Goodness is the sign of God within us.
It is our true worth.
We should never let anyone steal it from us.
We should never let anyone's words or actions erase the words
that God has inscribed in our hearts.

May our lips always be colored with the truth
and our eyes always be lined with compassion.
May our hands be beautified by the goodness of our deeds
and our minds be sweetened by humility.

Amma prays that all our lives may overflow with goodness.

The more water we draw from the well, the more the groundwater gushes.
The more we draw from our goodness, the more goodness arises.

May we cultivate goodness like a garden,
replenishing its soil every day with fresh water and nutrients.

May we pour out our Love with warm tears and sing out our sweetest feelings.

May we become someone who loves everyone.

May the selfless Love of pure Being shine from the hearts of Mother's children and illuminate the world.

13
QUIET MIND

Everything depends upon the mind.
When the mind is tranquil,
the deepest region of hell becomes a realm of happiness.
But when the mind is agitated, even the loftiest region of heaven
is a realm of sorrow.

We can always run away from an outer situation,
but we can never run away from our own mind.

Life circumstances are always changing.
Change is Nature's unchanging law.
What makes life bitter or sweet is our mind and attitude.

The ways of the mind are very strange—
we miss many things that are right in front of our eyes
and see many things that do not even exist.

People often do not perceive their blessings—
the blessing of human birth, the constant blessing of all-providing Nature.
We see the world not as it is, but as our mind is.
The Hindu scriptures call this *wrong vision.*

The world exists within us as thoughts and ideas.
"The world" is actually thought.

The mind is like wax and everything we think is impressed upon it.

As long as we cannot control our mind, sorrow keeps hunting us down.
But once the mind is under our control,
no problem or tragedy can devastate or immobilize us.

It is often said that the body is nothing but a sack of sorrow,
but the Ancients, who knew the Truth, experienced nothing but bliss.
From the worldly perspective the physical world is surely full of sorrow,
but sorrow is surmountable with spiritual practice.

The mind is nothing but a continuous flow of thoughts.
Our thoughts become our actions;
our actions become our habits;
and our habits become our personality.

The mind is nothing but a constant flow of thoughts.
And we, today, are its slaves.

The mind makes a good servant but not a good master!

If we give in to the mind too much and do no make any effort to control it,
we lose our mental balance and can even go mad.

Today all our minds are agitated.

The mind has become the noisiest place on Earth.

There is bumper-to-bumper traffic, inside as well as outside us.

Mental pollution has become one of the most serious problems in the world.

The mind is the greatest con artist in the world. It can sell us on any idea,
but cannot deliver on its promises.
And still we get hooked.

We are constantly thinking, daydreaming, trying to figure things out.
Thoughts jump from one thing to the next—and in them we dwell.
All this thinking creates the biggest impediment to remembering who we are.

Keep a close watch on the mind,
for it is a clever liar that hides our true nature and Self.

The mind has four aspects: *manas*, the faculty of perception;
chitta, the faculty of memory;
buddhi, the faculty of reason and intellect;
and *ahamkara*, the sense of I-ness or ego.

Our mental health depends upon how quiet we can keep the mind.

The mental faculties of thought and ego are the cause of our restlessness and agitation.

The mind creates problems and is a problem.

Society suffers from the disease of busy-ness and the epidemic keeps on spreading.
Jumping from one activity to the next, too busy to complete anything,
we get more and more dissatisfied and depressed.

Anxiety is the chief enemy,
our constant companion and a problem for everyone.
Analyzing it, we find that it is caused by worrying about the future
and obsessively reworking the past.

We want to be tension-free, but instead we take on free tension.

We minimize our physical activity and maximize our mental activity,
though our physical health depends on moving the body
and our mental health on quieting the mind.

Children, it is important to realize how harmful tension is
to both the mind and the body.
It is the root cause of most of our illnesses.

We worry unnecessarily about so many things and are chronically tense,
which reduces both our physical and mental stamina.

The only way out of this pattern is to surrender our burdens to the supreme Power.

The only reprieve from stress is surrender.
Since tension cannot be totally avoided, it is the only practical solution.

The tendency of the mind to doubt everyone and everything causes profound sorrow.

The mind naturally goes to extremes —
swinging between joy and sorrow, love and hate.
Only if we can learn to stay centered, will our thoughts abate.

Spiritual practice is necessary to learn to stay balanced.

The mind is the world's greatest traveler
and it takes a great deal of effort to learn to control it.

We should be able to control our minds as well as we control our bodies.

This is the function of meditation.

If the brain commands the feet to stop walking, they stop.
If it tells the hands to stop clapping, they stop.
If we ask the mind to stop, does it?
We should be able to stop the flow of thoughts in the mind — this is meditation.

We need to hold the remote control for the mind firmly in hand.

The mind must be on our side, and the only way to subdue it is through meditation.

We should not let our thoughts block our spiritual growth.

We need to meditate but lacking detachment, we do not feel like it.
To distance ourselves from the disturbances in and around us takes real effort!

The mind is basically lazy — its favorite past-times are eating and sleeping.

Any desire is basically a repetitive thought wave.

We create our thoughts and when we cooperate with them, we make them real.
If we withdraw our support, they will simply dissolve.

No thought has the power to control us.

The mind is like a giant supermarket with countless products we do not need.
We should not take all of them seriously, but try to focus instead.

Thought waves interfere with the experience of life.
As our thoughts subside, the mind becomes clearer, brighter and more stable.
Once the mind and the eye are calmer and subtler,
we can penetrate the surface of life.

We need to find the Silence in the noise,
which is difficult but not impossible.

A mind that is full of thoughts is ignorance.
A mind that is empty is truth.

Concentration is a colossal task—colossal as trying to dry out the ocean.
Nevertheless, try!
It is the only way to reach the goal.

To maneuver the ocean is not easy, my children.
But if we know the way and sincerely try, we will succeed.
On the boat of God, the deepest sea can be crossed.

As the mind is, so is the individual.
It is we who attribute reality to the unreal ego.
Take the ego for what it is—or is not—and forget about it.
Do not worry about bad thoughts, for the mind is nothing but a collection of thoughts.
Understand that they appear because it is time for them to disappear.

Just be careful not to identify with them.

As our thoughts diminish, the mind grows subtler and stronger.
As we become aware of our oneness with the universe
knowledge once obscure is made clear.

Everything is revealed to a mind that is peaceful.

The quieter the mind, the more it resembles the universal Mind.
The secrets of the universe are displayed upon the screen of a quiet mind.

Quiet meditative minds have given birth to innumerable wondrous discoveries and inventions.

To paint an inspiring picture, to write a moving poem, to study for an exam or ponder the mysteries of the universe, the mind must be still.
To gain higher Knowledge we must meditate.

Meditation is the art of quieting the mind.

Meditation helps us silence the mind.
And in that silence we can hear the voice of our true Self.

Thoughts and emotions feed the mind and become a burden
if we do not periodically unload them and relax.

If we do not unload our thoughts and emotions,
we cannot think or act properly—the mind becomes unbalanced.
Prayer, chant and meditation are ways to unload them.

As we contemplate pure Being, the waves of the mind naturally subside.

Normally the mind is lost in a profusion of thoughts.

Through meditation and mantra we learn to control the power of the mind and conserve, as well as increase, our energy.

Nothing in life can really be controlled but the mind.

With everything going on in the world today, the only way to stay sane is to make meditation an integral part of our daily lives.

The mind is madness and generates madness.

Meditation helps the mind to arrange, systematize and synthesize the seemingly random, chaotic flow of our thoughts.

Meditation can save us from all our agitation.

Meditation is the only way to master the mind and find the source of Silence within.

Meditation is like a filter that removes impurities from the mind.
In the mirror of a purified mind we can see ourselves, our thoughts and actions clearly.
We can easily distinguish right from wrong.

A meditative mind and spiritual knowledge are needed
to clarify and refine our thoughts and actions.

We need an even mind to lead a truly successful life.

May our failures never succeed in stopping us
from doing our spiritual practices.

Postponing our practices is like saying,
"I will go to the doctor when I feel better."

Spiritual practices, unlike many efforts to achieve worldly goals,
are never wasted and definitely bear fruit.

Baby steps are very important to our progress.

**In the beginning it is not good to force the mind to concentrate.
It is best to proceed gradually—preferably under the guidance of a master.**

**Sometimes out of sheer enthusiasm we can overdo spirituality.
Meditation affects the nervous system.
Excessive meditation can trigger convulsions and emotional disorders,
causing malfunction like any other over-heated device.
It is important to follow the advice of a master.**

**For people with mental problems, it is not advisable to meditate or chant for long.
Work unchallenging to the mind is more beneficial to their mental health.**

**Long inhalations and exhalations are safe—but even they should not be overdone.
Amma usually advises people to watch their breathing attentively,
since anyone can do this practice without harm.**

For beginning householders, it is sufficient to meditate
ten to thirty minutes twice a day.
After waking in the morning and at sunset are optimal times.
Under a guru's instruction, householders can meditate longer.

When we sleep we connect with the universal Energy.

When we sleep the true Self is eternally awake.

A good time for meditation is usually
between five in the evening and eleven in the morning.
Before going to bed at night, and after waking in the morning,
meditate while sitting on your bed.

Before meditating, bow to Mother Earth who embodies
the immortal virtues of patience, forbearance and generosity.

Even when we spit on her and gouge her with our metal plows and tools,
she tolerates and nourishes us, and offers us a place to rest.
Pray to absorb her virtues from your meditation.

Be courageous, children, bow to the Earth, and do your practices.

As you meditate, many thoughts enter the mind — this is the nature of the mind.
As you would pass many people on the street without engaging,
don't engage with every passing thought but hold your focus.
Do not worry about your thoughts — just keep practicing.

If you have a spiritual experience while meditating, do not take it too seriously —
it is only another dream.
If a beggar dreams he is a king — how will that benefit him when he wakes?
Try to maintain your balance in every waking moment —
that is a real accomplishment!

Yes, there are subtle beings invisible to the unsubtle mind
that we see when the mind is clearing and being refined by our practices —
but they are not important.
Ignore them and go beyond — they are nothing
compared to the Experience awaiting you.
Such trivial experiences are in fact obstacles on the path —
distractions from the true Reality.

If you gaze with a subtle eye, you will notice a hair-thin gap between thoughts.
If your thoughts are not allowed to run wild, the gap will increase —
but only if the mind stays focused on God.
Eventually all your thoughts and daydreams will disappear
and you will only think of God.

Every time the mind returns to God is meditation.
Every moment — and they are very few — we make contact with God
helps us progress on our journey.

We need to be steadfast in our practices.

There is no shortcut—practices have to be performed regularly and patiently.
After practicing, let them melt like sugar-candy in your mouth
and then swallow them.

After doing our practices, we need to give them time to sink in.
Forget the goal, your efforts and critiques of your progress—simply relax and be still.

Like a savings deposit that starts accruing interest immediately,
meditation and mantra bring immediate benefit to the practitioner.

**Our practices remain in our minds like embers among the coals
of an extinguished fire easily stirred and reignited.**

We are empowered by divine Energy!

Meditation is precious as pure gold: It brings prosperity,
peace of mind and elevation of the spirit.

Nothing is better than meditation.

Charging money for meditation
is like asking a baby to pay for its mother's milk.

Professionals still do not know the wonderful benefits
that meditation has to offer to all humanity.

Once we learn the art of relaxation
everything will become spontaneous and effortless!

Once we reclaim our mental power through spiritual practice
our patience will grow.

True meditation means Awareness of every thought, word and deed.

We must try to be alert and aware of all our actions
and meditation is the easiest way.

Meditation does not simply mean closing your eyes
and sitting motionless in one posture—it means tapping into That
which sustains all thought, word and action.

Meditation is the way to close the doors and windows of the senses
and gaze within and see our own true Self.

Look within, observe your thoughts and trace them to their Source.
Remember that you are pure Being, Awareness and Bliss.

Dropping all your regrets about the past, simply relax
and you will feel stronger and more alive.

When relaxed, we can glimpse our true nature —
the infinite source of Existence itself.

When you cannot control your unhappiness,
meditate, chant a mantra or read some holy scripture.
This will help you quiet your mind and avoid wasting time and harming your health.

Mantra repetition is another tool that aids in controlling the mind
and improving our physical and mental health.
The purpose of mantra is to tame the mind.
The mind travels millions of miles per second and is very difficult to control.
Mantra can be chanted anywhere —
when walking, bathing, eating, or doing any other activity.

In the dark Age of Materialism, saying a mantra while inhaling and exhaling —
first with the lips, then mentally — is the easiest way to achieve
inner purification and concentration.

A mantra received from a totally pure guru has a transformative power.
It is like yoghurt stirred into milk — infused with divine Energy, it works internally.

The name of God is powerful —
and chanted with concentration, it is even more powerful!

We can use our mantra like a cell phone to call God at any time.

Mantra chanting can take us to the threshold of absolute Reality —
from which point we can easily cross over.

Even mantra chanted mechanically are beneficial.

Mantra repetition and meditation on one's favorite deity are good spiritual practices.
We can repeat our mantra between tasks
or gaze at our deity, then close our eyes and picture it internally.

Amma gives mantra initiation to anyone who requests it
in the hopes that it will be chanted occasionally, even if not continuously,
and grant some benefit—which is Amma's only concern.

Amma sows the seed—maybe it will sprout—in this lifetime or the next.

In Buddhism, devotional practices such as initiation, prostration, visualization of deities,
chanting, rituals and rites are performed to help the practitioner develop
a pure idea or image for meditation.

If you have faith in Amma, you can meditate on Her.
If you worship Mary or Christ, meditate on Them.
If you have no favorite deity, meditate on a flame or a point.
If you love Nature, you can meditate on the Moon—
or imagine merging into a river or a lake or the beautiful incandescent sky.
Or imagine that you are God and meditate on That.
The most important thing is your concentration.

We do not need to believe in God to achieve liberation —
we can simply imagine dissolving into the Infinite
like a river pouring into the ocean.

It is good for any seeker to gaze into the endless bliss of space.

Gazing up at the sky, picture your Beloved moving alongside you.
See your Beloved's face in the Moon, feel her caress in the wind.
Imagine your Beloved calling, kissing, hugging, stroking and blessing you —
playing peek-a-boo in the clouds!
Going deeper into your Consciousness, hold the Beloved enshrined
in your expanding heart as you move closer and closer
to your own true Self.

Our goal is mastery of the mind.
Many kinds of spiritual practices can lead us to that goal.
Amma rejects none of them.
They have been transmitted to us by great Seers not fools.

They could see God in all forms and therefore utilized many practices
to focus the mind.

The point of all modes of spiritual practice is to help us learn
the great lesson of letting go.

Ritual is one more way to focus on cosmic Consciousness
and gain control of our minds.
Like mantra and prayer, it purifies.

The mind tends to focus on the bad—that is why it is so important to chant and pray.

To rid ourselves of negative feelings and maintain the right spirit
we must meditate, pray and contemplate—and never allow thoughts
of any kind to block our spiritual advancement.

When we go deep enough, we can see that all spiritual practices—

even singing to ourselves—are ways that God opens us to the Truth.

Meditation, chanting, singing and mantra are all invitations
to the Divine to reveal itself.

God is the uninvited guest waiting at the door of every heart.
Whether we invite God in, or even know It is there, God is always present—
hidden in everything, giving it its beauty, making it what it is.
This is the hidden formula of life—revealed and known only if we search for It.

The uninvited Guest will never appear without invitation.
In every cranny of the world, in every inch of space,
in every gap between atoms It waits.
There is no place where It is not — It is everywhere.
We only need to notice It.
It will never break in aggressively, for It is Love.
It is not a person but Consciousness itself.
When you invite It in, Love and Consciousness will enter.

Otherwise, out of pure compassion, It will keep waiting.

If you wish to invite the Guest in, prayer and meditation are the way to do it.

Prayer invites God in.

When we pray, we enter into a dialogue with our own true Self.

God needs to be invoked through prayer.

No other practice gives us the bliss of divine Love as well as sincere prayer.
Just call from your heart like a child crying to be fed, held and cuddled by its mother.
If you call with that intensity and innocence, She will reveal Herself—
She cannot remain silent and unmoved.
The state reached by calling and crying out to God
is as great as the bliss of the yogi in samadhi.

Whatever you are doing, talk to your Beloved, pour out your problems and sorrows—
in Whom else should you confide?

Instead of multiplying your problems by sharing them with others,
share them with God—and try to solve them.
This will eventually bring you some peace.

Let prayer and remembrance become a part of your daily life.

We should remember the Divine and chant our mantra while doing our tasks
to avoid becoming enslaved to earthly pleasure.

Keep talking to God and increasingly you will feel God's presence
until it eventually becomes constant.

Constant remembrance of God is true devotion.

As our imagination and our resolve grow stronger and stronger, we will gradually experience the presence of God within and around us.

The intensity of the longing for God
is like two birds perched on different branches
swaying, whenever the leaves block their view, to avoid losing eye contact.

True devotion is remembrance of God everywhere and always.
If we always remember God, God will come.

Tears of devotion are more powerful than any meditation.

Spiritual devotion is the pure flow of innocent Love for God.

The sweetness and bliss of desireless devotion is utterly unique.
Although non-dual Advaita is the ultimate Truth,
sometimes Mother feels it is all meaningless and She would rather simply be
an innocent child before God.

The zenith of devotion is perfect Love.

Devotion to any object or task is very important
and involves simultaneous focus on and awareness of our Oneness.

When we love, the mind constantly streams toward the object of our Love.
Love demands concentration, and concentration demands Love.
Intense concentration nurtures the evolution of Love.

The Kali Yuga, the current age of Materialism,
and the entire cycle of ages are all actually within us.
Amma says, with the right attitude we will always find time to think of God.
We can focus our minds on God in any age — attitude is the key.

Bhajans are songs of prayer rich in meaning and devotion.
When we sing them wholeheartedly, we can lose ourselves in our longing for God —
which is what true meditation is.

There is nothing like the bliss of singing the divine Name!
It is so fulfilling that Mother would never hesitate to incarnate simply to do that.
Even those who reach the Ultimate come down to sing the glories of God.

Devotional singing relieves the mind and gives us tremendous joy!
To receive the maximum benefit one should immerse oneself
in the feeling that I am nothing and You are everything.

Children, the mind should be an elevator that rises straight to God.

The purer our minds become, the more we can manifest our own divinity.
We are all divine but a pure heart can express it more fully!
Spiritual practices, like meditation and service, are crucial to purifying our minds.

Once our minds are purified, we can experience others' pain and joy as our own.

The purpose of all spiritual practice is to develop a mind that allows us
to give ourselves fully to the world.

The mind is like dust in the eye—a foreign object that needs to be removed
if we are ever to know perfection, bliss and contentment.

The goal of spiritual life is to gain control of the mind and go beyond it!

What is the mind but all our accumulated unhappiness, negativity and discontent?
The ego is never satisfied—how can we ever find happiness with such a mind?
The harder we try, the unhappier we become.
We are happy only when the mind and all its egocentric thoughts are gone.

The mind creates both sorrow and happiness—
and sorrow is the only obstacle to our happiness.
To enjoy life we have to forget ourselves—and to do that
we must have good control of the mind.

The nature of the mind is to calculate, but whenever we calculate
we lose the benefit of our sacrifice.

We have to declare open war on the mind.
When pushed and pulled into the same old ruts,
remember, the world's greatest Trickster
is trying to pull you off track—and do not give up!

At some point your negative tendencies will give way
and Reality will rush in and take over.

When we finally free ourselves from the mind and wake up,
we will feel like drunks drying out after a long binge.

To be free of the mind, we have to change the quality of our thoughts.
Good thoughts help us fix the mind on God.
We need to replace our negative thoughts with thoughts of God.

Negative thoughts are eliminated
by cultivating and developing good thoughts.

Good thoughts purify our blood, mind, memory, intellect, and health.
Evil thoughts destroy them.

An ordinary person can blossom into a spiritual person through spiritual practice,
through a selfless attitude and positive thinking.

Learning to focus the mind,
we can increase our spiritual power.

As ice becomes more subtle and forceful when it melts,
the mind becomes more subtle and forceful when it focuses—
allowing us to accomplish anything.

Conditions are forever changing.
Happiness is forever alternating with unhappiness.
Let us try to cultivate an attitude of equanimity and acceptance.

Let us try to be like the river and say Yes to everything.

Change is a natural part of life—we should be ready
to accept any situation in life with a smile.
Acceptance is the key to our success.

Spirituality is receptivity—
the ability to accept experiences without reacting.

Expectations—like sorrow—are something we ourselves create.

The mind always creates expectations.
To be truly conscious we have to let them go.

Every reaction slows our progress toward the goal of Self-realization,
while acceptance draws a steady flow of grace toward us.

True spirituality is reflected in the ability to be calm, patient and forgiving.
When we have this ability, the mind remains tranquil.
Spirituality is a quiet mind — a state of Silence.

Peace is the deep feeling that engulfs the heart when thoughts of the past disappear.
Peace is not the opposite of distress but its total absence.
Peace is total relaxation and rest.

The mind and the heart must become one
for divine Grace to grant us peace.

Think of your mind as a lake and your thoughts as the ripples on the surface.
A meditative mind is like a lotus floating on a glassy lake.

The soil in which meditation flourishes is Love.

Receptivity arises from Love,
which makes us simple and open as a child.

Only Love can silence the mind.
In a state of pure Love we are silent—at peace in the Supreme Self.

Silence is the language of Love.

God speaks to us in the language of Silence.
When our thoughts subside and the mind is calm,
we can hear the melody of God.
God sees and knows all our thoughts, actions, silences and everything else
since we dwell in her infinite Shakti—her divine Energy.

All our thoughts and actions exist within God.

The real aim of all spiritual practices is to develop a heart
that is overflowing with Love for all.

Reducing our thoughts makes room for Love's energy to flow through us.

True meditation is an uninterrupted flow of contemplation on Divinity.

Once the mind is purified by meditation,
every atom becomes a form for meditation.

Meditative practices give us the power and courage to smile kindly
even at Death — to see Life as a delightful play
and experience death as bliss.

When we behold the entire universe as the blissful play of divine Consciousness —
what can we do but smile?

Meditation takes us to the state of no mind, no ego — the state beyond death and birth.
When we transcend the mind, we transcend death.

Without the mind, there is no world.
With the mind, there are many names and forms.
Once the mind is gone, there is nothing—neither sleep nor wakefulness.
We are not aware of any objective existence—only perfect stillness, peace and bliss.

Meditation is the saving grace that bestows immortality and eternity.

In the end, it is the mind that bestows bliss.

A quiet mind is the key to human fulfillment.

The mind creates both our happiness and our unhappiness
and when we have finally understood this,
our work is done.

A peaceful mind is our true wealth.

Pray for a peaceful contented mind, no matter what happens.
This is the one true Prayer.

Though the Sun is millions of miles away, the Lotus blossoms.
Pray sincerely and God will hear you —
never mind when, where or how.
God is in your own mind.

With sincere effort and prayer,
we can invoke the grace of Universal Consciousness.

When we truly pray, there is nothing to ask, demand or suggest.
True prayer is sincere, utter surrender.

A quiet inner world is an abode of peace and joy.

May there be peace on Earth.
May there be peace all around and within us.
Om Shanti, Shanti, Shanti.

14
DISCRIMINATION

To human beings the Goddess gave a boon
She gave to no other creature: the power of discrimination.
To ignore this boon is to throw away your life.

Humanity considers itself the Crown of Creation,
but its real superiority lies in the power of discriminative intelligence.
Only when this power is used to attain higher Consciousness do we become worthy
of the title, since other creatures are in many ways superior to us.

Self-discipline and Self-knowledge are what make us human.
Without these, we are barely different from worms.

If human beings do not use the discernment that allows them to seek the truth,
how can we ever be considered superior to animals?
Worms and other animals are born, work, procreate and die.
If we live the same way they do, what is the difference between us?
What message do we leave to the world?

True understanding comes from a discerning, discriminating mind.

There are lessons to be learned from every experience in life,
but it takes careful attention and discernment
to see what life is trying to teach us.

There is infinite Power in everyone, but few are aware of this.
Born in suffering, we live and die in suffering.
Our inner Self constantly speaks to us — softly, clearly and lovingly.
But we are too impatient to listen.
We repeat the same mistakes over and over.
And so we continue to suffer.

Happiness is within us, and the longer we seek it outside us,
the more frustrated we get.
At some point we realize that our life is in danger
and the only thing we can depend on is the power of the Universe.
The fear that Death will take everything from us, drives us to search for a way out.
Eventually we discover the spiritual path that leads to the only power
that can ever conquer Death.

Right now we have God at the bottom of the list, but God should be at the top!
If we put God first, the other things will fall into place.
But if we put the world first, God will not follow.
We are free to choose—the bottom or the top.

We have to choose between temporary happiness that leads to endless unhappiness;
or temporary unhappiness that leads to eternal peace.

We have to develop the patience and ability to discriminate
between the transitory and the Eternal.

We need to exercise our faculty of discrimination
to determine the right path of action.

Actions that lead to God are righteous or dharmic.
Actions that do not lead to God are unrighteous or adharmic.
For the intellect, the difference between right and wrong is a line drawn on water.

The path of Dharma is the only path on which we cannot fail.

My children, we should carefully avoid any wrong action
that will block the flow of grace into our lives.
Having the freedom to decide how to act, we should exercise it
and choose the right action and the right attitude.

Honing the intellect with discrimination
and using it to observe yourself strengthens the mind.

Information must evolve into knowledge
and knowledge into discrimination.

Only the human mind can mature and become immortal,
but that potential can only be realized by walking the path of Consciousness.

If we can become aware of the consequences of our actions,
we will not do the wrong thing.
We make mistakes because we are not aware.

Discernment is a constant process of listening,
contemplating our conscience and putting it into action.

Our conscience is the coat that protects and warms us when the weather turns cold.

Try to be patient and discriminate between the ephemeral and the Eternal.

Discrimination turns on the light of true Knowledge.

We were born to be happy, but with happiness also come
responsibility and right action.
Everything in this world has a dharma or a duty.

Before doing something,
we should ask ourselves whether it is right or wrong.
And if it is wrong we should not do it.

The mind only understands the language of the ego
which generates our desires.
We should listen to our conscience and our heart.

The intellect cannot discriminate between sand and sugar when mixed,
but the heart, like an ant, goes straight for the sugar—and that is its beauty.
We need to learn the language of the heart.

We should be discriminating with every word and action.

The nature of this world is change—there are always times
when life is smooth and times when life is rough.
All of us have the discriminatory power to determine whether a situation
is one we should try to change, or one we should try to accept.

The cosmic Power that creates and organizes the universe
has created guidelines for humanity called Dharma.
Dharma has rhythm, tone and melody,
and when we fail to think and act in accordance with it,
the balance between the human mind and Nature is lost.

For the traffic of life to flow smoothly, we have to follow the rules.
If we do not follow the rules, it is not God who is responsible.
When a doctor prescribes a medication and we ignore the directions,
drink the whole bottle and harm our health—how can we blame the doctor?

When we drive carelessly and have an accident, can we blame the gasoline?
Can we blame God for the problems we cause through our own ignorance?
God has made it clear how to live on this earth—
it is pointless to blame God when we do not follow the instructions.

Everything has a dharma—its own basic nature and correct code of conduct.
If we do not follow our dharma, if we turn away and simply act on our desires,
we compromise and eventually destroy our own character.

Think of all the painful psychological blows you have received
until finally you became a big walking wound.
Why did this happen? Because of your poor judgment—
because you failed to use your discrimination.

Life offers us no warranties or guarantees, only circumstances and opportunities.
Because of its dual nature, life is unstable and tenuous, and cannot offer us safety.
What it does offer is the opportunity to rise — by means of discrimination — to our higher Self.

Do not miss the precious opportunity to find your eternally blissful Self by running after fleeting pleasures.

Whatever we see, hear or experience in this world is ephemeral.
Get in touch with the eternal bedrock of everything.

Always remember that everything that exists, is the divine Self and highlight That rather than the temporal body.

Once we awaken to divine Consciousness we will realize that this world is only a dream.

Birth and death are the basic features of life—
the two pillars that support the bridge of Life.
They do not ask our permission or consider our requests.
They are neither under our control, nor subject to our understanding.
How, then, can we conceivably lay claim to a life that operates
independently of our own wishes?

No one can stop fate—if something is meant to happen,
it will happen and cannot be prevented.

Things do not happen because we will them.
Not even this moment, much less the next, is under our control.
There is no guarantee of even one more breath.

Only through discrimination can we understand the message
hidden behind both positive and negative experiences
and accept whatever happens with a smile.

Let us use the body profitably to seek and find the Soul.
That is the point of life.

We should eat to live and sleep to awaken—not the reverse.

Only if we go beyond the taste of the tongue will we ever
taste the sweetness of the heart.

It takes real strength of mind to say no to pleasures—
spirituality is for the courageous!

Spiritual success demands patience, awareness and a discerning mind.

We should try to develop discrimination in everything we do.
Only such actions will succeed.

Instruct the mind, "Oh Mind, why do you crave
all these unnecessary things that never satisfy you,
that drain your energy and always make you restless and tense?
Can't you stop all this wandering, return to your blissful Source
and finally rest in peace?"

Creation is taking place inside each of us.
Every mind is a small world created by our thoughts.
Our thoughts develop into desires that perpetuate the whole cycle all over again.

Only human beings have the capacity to convert good into bad and bad into good.

We should be careful with every word we say
because through our words new worlds are being created.

Words are incredibly powerful.

In the beginning, before Creation,
there was total Silence—the silence of Peace.
The cosmic Mind was in a state of total absorption.
Then the Word, the first word, broke that Silence and the world was born.

Children, we should be careful with every word.
From a word, this world came into being—it was founded on a word!
We should speak very carefully.

We should express kindness in every word and action—
but most of us lack the necessary discrimination.

Actions performed unconsciously as well as those performed consciously bear fruit.

Life is like a game whose outcome cannot be known until the very end—
we must pay close attention to every single move.

Do not let the opinions of others sway you.
The first step on the path is satsang—relations with those who share your beliefs.

It is very important to spend your time with people of a similar philosophy
when walking the spiritual path.

Friendship is like an elevator that can take you up or down.
Choose your friends wisely!

It is easy to embrace the world, but after the honeymoon always comes the sorrow.
To keep God with us may be challenging at first, but if we persist
we will attain everlasting happiness and banish sorrow.

When we experience conflict between our worldly dharma and our higher dharma,
we should always choose our higher dharma for the good of the world.

Only pure actions today will yield a good tomorrow.

The result of yesterday's action is today's fate.

The pain and sorrow that we experience in difficult times
is the consequence of our past actions.

Our conscience records everything.
We can never escape the court of our own conscience.

All our thoughts and actions pass through God.

The results of our actions are like income tax — it is pointless to try to explain,
"I was really in a difficult place that day."

Do not get depressed over what happened — what is done is done.
But try to live your future moments with discrimination.

If we do a hundred good things and make one mistake, people hate and reject us.
But if we make a hundred mistakes and do one good thing,
God will love and accept us.

Depend only on God.
Dedicate everything to God.

The purpose of life is to experience and realize our own divinity.
This is the message spoken in countless languages by all the teachers, sages and seers
given to humanity down through the ages.

The two most important days of our lives
are the day we were born and the day we realize why we were born.

The reason we were born is to know who we are
and to help others.
Never forget this!

Our highest and most important duty in this world
is to help our fellow beings.

It is not enough to simply be individuals.
We need to become conscious individuals.
This is the reason for spirituality.

Whether God exists, is not the question.

Try to view every experience in life as a stepping-stone to growth and fulfillment
and approach life with a discriminating spiritual attitude.

Discriminative intelligence is a slow steady process that unfolds within each of us
like a bud opening into a flower.

Centered in Love, we should cultivate discrimination
in every aspect of our daily lives.

Every new year is a fresh new page in the Book of Life.
On it, we can write whatever we wish —
words of Love, compassion, peace and wisdom,
or words of hatred, anger and darkness.
Let us fill our pen of discrimination with the ink of effort
and write something fresh and new on each page.

We can only experience as much newness and freshness in our lives
as there is Love within us.
If the light of Love is not present, even in new things
we will only experience darkness.

God's supreme gifts to humanity are Love and discrimination.
If we use them wisely, we can know God.

Discrimination is the switch that turns on the lamp of Enlightenment.

15
DETACHMENT

We brought nothing into this world when we came
and will take nothing with us when we go—not even a pin.
We need to become detached from worldly things,
which cannot provide lasting happiness.

Although everything is God,
we perceive things around us as separate
and feel attraction towards some, and repulsion towards others.
As a result, joy and sorrow are the nature of life.

Once we free ourselves from our likes and our dislikes,
God will shine from our hearts.

We need to understand and accept that the world is full of pain
and become aware and detached.

When we go to the zoo, we enjoy the wild lions and tigers from a distance,
understanding that it is dangerous to go too close.
We should always maintain an inner distance from outer events.

Today we are ruled by our desires —
enslaved by our likes and dislikes, attachments and repulsions.
In this state, how can we ever be peaceful and happy?

Everything we cling to, every desire we satisfy,
is a shore where we sought peace and tranquility
and were once again disappointed.

Those who depend on material and transitory objects are deeply disappointed.

Depending on things that change, foreshadows unhappiness.

Everything is constantly changing — we need to really understand this.
If we do not, we will suffer.

Every time we step into the river, the water is different.

Today's newspaper is tomorrow's wastepaper.

Today's criminal may be tomorrow's saint.
Today's friend may be tomorrow's foe and today's foe tomorrow's friend.
Our mind too is constantly changing —
one day we like someone, the next day we don't.
This is the nature of the mind.

In Amma's childhood, women repaired torn clothing—they stitched the tears
and patched the holes—it was painful to see anyone in rags.
Today blue jeans cost twenty-five dollars but we pay a hundred dollars
for jeans with patches and holes added.
Clothes ironically expose parts of the body they were originally designed to conceal,
and torn clothes no longer cause shame.

People once suffered from starvation,
but today they starve on purpose to lose a few pounds.
We used to feel ashamed of not having food and clothing,
but today we take pride in starving ourselves and wearing rags—
what once caused shame confers prestige!
Some people mock a woman with a hunched back,
but when a designer puts a bulge on the back of a dress it is chic!
It is all in the mind.

We identify with what we see, when we should identify
with the One who sees.

We need to step back and witness.

Thinking comes from the mind and witnessing from the higher Self—
from a state of pure Consciousness.
The mind and its thoughts are unreal fictions that we create.
Thinking is false and Consciousness is true.

The mind—like our name—was given to us at birth
and over time we became more and more identified with it.
But the mind exists no more than darkness, which is merely the absence of light.

The world is not the problem—the problem lies in the mind.
Be watchful and you will see with greater clarity.
Watchfulness produces a penetrating eye and mind so we cannot be deceived,
and slowly takes us closer to the true being of the blissful Self.

Try to develop the ability to step back and witness the thoughts that pass through your mind and your mind will become stronger.

To be a witness really means waking up
and becoming conscious of everything going on in and around us.

Caught in the drama of life, we experience so much suffering,
but when we witness life, we are not affected.

Witness Consciousness, the true I, remains unaffected and untouched.
It is constant, free and detached.

True witnessing is pure bliss.

In this changing world only one thing is changeless, the Self,
and based on That, all change takes place.
Wake up to this state of mind!
Our human purpose is to realize the changeless Self.

We should view the world as a temporary stop on a journey.
Traveling on a train, we encounter many passengers.
We talk and share our thoughts on life, and sometimes become attached.
But every passenger has to disembark at his or her destination.
When you meet someone and begin to settle in, remember that one day you must part.
By strengthening this awareness and maintaining a positive attitude,
you will be able to survive anything.

There are three rings in this world:
the engagement ring, the wedding ring, and the suffering.

Because of attachment we suffer, and once attachment sneaks in
even the purest Love changes into suffering.

We mistake attachment for Love.

Human beings love out of desire —
only the true and ultimate Self can love selflessly.

Human beings do not love selflessly.
In ordinary love, there is always expectation,
insincerity, impurity and conditionality.

The world is full of sorrow — people love selfishly, not selflessly.
Even our relations love us to fulfill their own needs.
Only God can love us selflessly.

Only God can love us without expecting anything in return.
Even the great Souls immersed in God occasionally experience attachment.

Children, the love the world offers us leads to suffering.
We imagine that others' love will make us happy, but happiness does not come
from anything external — it comes from within.

We can live without attachment, but not without Love.

Even if every creature in the world loved us,
it would only amount to a tiny fraction of the blissful Love
constantly flowing from God.
Worldly love can never compare with absolute Love.

Worldly love is inconstant—it fluctuates and finally fades.
At first it is exciting and beautiful, but eventually it becomes shallow
and usually it ends in disappointment, animosity and pain.
Spiritual Love, on the other hand, is fathomless and measureless.
Lasting peace and happiness are born of divine Love
and the knowledge that Creation is One.

All around the world people say, "I love you."
Instead we should say, "I am Love."

In "I love you," Love gets crushed between "you" and "I".

Real Love is unconditional, spontaneous and unforced.
When we experience the other as separate, we tend to push,
but when we experience our Oneness, conditions are irrelevant and force is pointless.
We are simply a passageway through which Life's energy is flowing.

When we taste sugar as something separate from us, we taste the sweetness—
but we should become the Sweetness.

Only when we open our minds and abandon the narrow viewpoint of the *I*,
can God be expressed through us completely.

Only if we expand our perspective, can we understand this truth.

All forms of love are one Love.

Search for the eternal Self, the real source of happiness,
and learn to be satisfied with what you have.
If we can renounce greed, selfishness and jealousy,
we will reach the end of all our desiring.

Mother realizes that renouncing desires is especially hard for Western children,
but if we can remember the fleeting nature of material things
while living amid so many temptations, and understand that such pleasures
are hollow and incapable of providing real inner happiness, we will not succumb.

Desirelessness is the true measure of spiritual greatness.
Let us try to free ourselves from all attachment.

Attachment occurs because we perceive other beings as separate
and different from ourselves.
Once we understand that everything belongs to God,
we will not become attached.

Try to become a witness.

Life is a combination of happiness and sorrow.
Like the pendulum of a clock, it swings back and forth from one side to the other.

Do not be attached—the ability to stay unattached
in the present moment is true balance.

Detachment does not just come naturally.

No one reaches the heights without preparation.
Without making an effort and learning detachment,
we will never become strong enough.
Anyone who wants to expand their potential and experience peace
must practice detachment.

Detachment means witnessing the experiences of life.

When we are aware of the fireworks around us, the next loud bang will not startle us.
When we are conscious of the nature of this world, we will not lose our balance.

Life swings like a pendulum between fortune and misfortune,
pausing at one side just long enough to gain the momentum to swing to the other side.
When you are fortunate and comfortable, always remember that it is momentary—
new challenges are on the way.

Prepare your mind—try to accept and surrender.
Welcome both the good and the bad and face death with a smile.
This is the only way to contentment.

The principle of spirituality teaches us to accept both happiness
and unhappiness with equanimity.
We can only do this by surrendering to God.
Do not become euphoric when happy, or devastated when sad.

When you succeed, realize that it is divine grace and deepen your surrender.
When you fail, find out why, correct your mistakes, and renew your effort.
If you keep trying and failing, console yourself that this is God's will.

Try to accept everything, both good and bad, as divine will.

Face life with few expectations and no assumptions.

Too much expectation is not good—it causes problems.
Be attached but not unhappy.

Whatever the outer circumstances, try to remain peaceful and calm.

In detachment, there is no anger or expectation.

When others throw dirt at us in the form of unpleasant words or actions,
we should try to shake it off.

A truly spiritual person is like the wind that blows over flowers and feces alike.

Detachment preserves the sweet scent of the holy.

Stay detached—reflecting and releasing like a mirror.

Serve with detachment—without feeling *it is I who am doing this*.
Understand that it is God that makes you serve.

Always remember that God is the force behind everything you do.

Before you act, surrender the action to God.
Do not think, *It is I who am doing this*.
Be aware that it is only because of the supreme Power that you act and have the strength to do so.

Move on, in the assumption that everything is ordained by God.
Whenever we do that, we will feel peace.

Actions should be performed without attachment
and with the understanding that God acts through us.

Detachment is another word for skillful action.

While you work, cultivate the attitude of detachment —
as if you were floating like butter on water.
Imagine God working through you, and the work will not bind you.
Be a conduit.

As you do each thing, feel the energy flowing from the Supreme Self,
without which no thought or action can happen.

We are neither the planter nor the harvester.

The Supreme acts through all our actions —
do not become attached to the outcome.

As we sow the seeds, they may sprout or not.
Leave it to God.

Try to free yourself from attachment to the result.

When we invest in the stock market,
we understand that we can either make or lose money.
Cultivate the attitude of accepting either potential.
This is what detachment means: understanding the dual nature of the world,
accepting either possibility, and moving on.

Life should be like swinging on a swing.
There are always ups and downs.
Accept everything as it is.

External circumstances constantly change: fortune alternates with adversity.
Consciously cultivate the attitude of complete acceptance
and you will find your peace and joy.
Make detachment your best friend.

The greatest of all riches is contentment.
Always try to be content with what you have.

Do not desire what you do not have, covet what others have,
and minimize others' pain by thinking you would be happier in their shoes,
which is simply not true since every individual has problems and worries.
We cannot exchange our own problems for another's
and would not be able to bear their pain even if we could.

If you think your neighbor is happier than you and wish be like him,
then actually experienced his life — you would discover how wrong you were.

Your neighbor's joy and pain are his, as your joy and pain are yours.
Try to understand this and become content with what you have.
You cannot have more or less than you have.
What you have is meant for you.

Along with more wealth and comfort come more worries and problems.
Along with more desires comes more discontent.
Desires are endless and so is the chain of greed and selfishness.
Learn to be content with what you have.

Contentment means surrender and complete acceptance,
the ability to welcome every experience in life with an open mind
and to smile even at Death.

The only way to reach the eternal Truth is to cultivate an attitude of surrender.

Accepting both good and bad is true spirituality.

The sign of a true devotee is the smile of acceptance on one's face.

Be willing to surrender to the supreme Will.

Perform all your actions without attachment.

Be like a pipeline connected to Love with no expectations at all.

Let every action be an act of worship and learn to see God in everything you do.

See God in everyone.

We should be able to see every atom of this world as Truth
and serve it with equanimity, composure and serenity—these are the qualities of God.

A great householder leads a life of detachment,
renounces everything and surrendersto God,
accepting every experience, good or bad, as a divine blessing.

A great householder understands that worldly relationships are temporary
and functions without any sense of ownership.
A humble faithful servant serves until told to stop.

May you always see everything as divine Consciousness
and serve That selflessly.

Renounce ownership
and realize that everything belongs to God.

Renounce and enjoy,
for the real fruit, the real happiness is already inside you.
Learn how to satisfy yourself with experiencing That.

Once you are totally detached, you can truly respond.
This will happen only when you can free yourself from the mind and the ego—
which are only able to react and cannot really respond.

Reacting to a situation postpones the attainment of Self-realization,
while accepting it invites a steady stream of grace.

The suffering in this world is caused by the ego.
There is no suffering in God's world.

As the intellect develops, the ego—the sense of I and mine—
also develops, making it harder to surrender.

Only when we can feel how much our attachments burden us
can we experience the relaxation and bliss of detachment and renunciation.

Where there is no desire, there is no suffering.

The ego is the only thing a human being creates on his or her own.

Once it is surrendered, only divine Creation exists.
We are simply a flute on God's lips.

The purpose of every human birth is to know God as the true Self—
and this can only happen if we surrender the ego.

We can truly respond only when we are empty
and do not wish to disturb the silence with unnecessary sounds
or mar the blank page with unnecessary words.
A true response arises spontaneously from a loving heart.

We need to outgrow our individuality in order to merge in universal Love.

We should gaze up into space—beyond motion, form and quality—into infinite bliss.
Knowing that I am the embodiment of pure being, awareness and bliss,
take the essence and shed the rest.

Just as blossoms fall when the fruit ripens,
worldly cravings fade as our detachment grows.

Once we realize the triviality of our worldly attachments
and the sublimity of our Love for God, we will shed our attachments
like fading flowers yielding to the fruit.

The shedding of desires, like the shedding of leaves,
is a sign that soon we too will blossom.
Spiritual progress is subtle.

As situations and experiences unfold, new and unknown phases of life
keep presenting themselves, taking us ever closer to our true Self.
It is only a matter of time.

Worldly desire dissipates as detachment evolves.
Whether we live in a house or a forest we will eventually become free of all desire.

If God-realization is our goal, nothing else will matter.
We will know that nothing physical lasts and bliss is only found within.

Bliss never comes from the outside—it only comes from the inside.
When we contemplate this deeply, and truly become detached,
the mind will stop running after illusory pleasure.

Illusion does not mean non-existence, but change.
Nirvana does not mean the extinction of the world.
We do not deny the existence of the world.
We want to be aware of its true nature—to realize
that it is ever changing, and there exists another greater Reality.

Dedication, knowledge and detachment are necessary
to fully realize our true Self.

We need steadfastness as our path,
discrimination as our guide
and detachment as our guardian.

Amma says, with persistent effort we will finally reach the goal.
We are not subtle enough yet to gauge our spiritual progress.
Like someone flying in an airplane, we cannot tell how fast we are flying.

May Mother's children enjoy the Consciousness
that empowers us to always smile with faith in the Supreme Being.
May we learn to perform our actions as an assigned duty
without identifying with them.

Like a bird perched on a dry twig, prepare to spread your wings
and fly with the wind when the twig breaks.
Living in this world, always remember the eternal Truth
and nourish Love in your hearts.

Liberation from sorrow is not something we attain after death in some other world.
It is something that has to be understood and experienced
while we are alive in this world.

The Creator's life-giving power informs all things.
Liberation is the ability to see the divine Glory and infinite Power
that dwells in everything — not only in the good and the beautiful
but also in the bad and the ugly.

Once we can see that life and all it brings is an extremely precious gift,
we can say *Yes* and accept everything.

Happiness comes from the mind's capacity to adapt to any situation.
It is within not outside us.

Happiness never comes only from physical comfort — it comes from going inward,
nurturing our spiritual awareness, and learning how to control the mind.

We alone decide how we will use our minds.

We alone create our expectations and disappointments.

It is we who make our lives either bitter or sweet.

Happiness is a choice like any other.

May we firmly decide that whatever happens we will be happy and strong.
We are not alone — God is always with us.

Remember: God is with me, I have the power to do anything!

If we surrender, we will be blessed with success.

To be happy and content, forget about happiness and contentment.
Stop living in the past and the future, and abandon the search for happiness.

A truly spiritual person is like a river, within and without,
forever offering peace and Love — flowing onward unattached.

We should try to be accepting.
The more accepting we are, the more fearless
and the more loving we will be — since we have no expectations.

Darling children, say *Yes* to life,
say *Yes* to everything!
To accept is to say *Yes*.
Even when everything seems to be going wrong,
be like the river and say *Yes*, I accept.

The river of life will always carry you — Love simply flows.

Anyone who wishes to dive in, is always welcome.
Anyone who wishes to take the plunge, will be accepted unconditionally.

Divine Consciousness permeates the cool breeze,
the vast sky and the beautiful full Moon.
It permeates all beings and all things.
To realize this is the goal of life.
Children, be like the sky—
be vast and peaceful and all embracing.

Love is the center of life—attachment is only the periphery.
May we lead our lives focused on Love and aim for the very Center!

Understanding the nature of this changing world
and remaining centered in ourselves,
we should love one another.
This is right attachment.

**Right attachment is detachment,
and right detachment is attachment.**

Perceiving others as Oneself is true detachment.

**Always act from the center of Love
within you.**

JANINE CANAN MD, psychiatrist and poet, graduate of Stanford University *with distinction* and New York University School of Medicine, has followed Mata Amritanandamayi for three decades and authored many books of poetry, translations, anthologies, stories and essays, including compilations of Amma's teachings — the award-winning *Messages from Amma: In the Language of the Heart, Garland of Love,* and *Love Is My Religion.*

PRAISES FOR AMMA

"God's Love in a human body." — Conservationist Jane Goodall

"A supernova of spirituality!" — *Hinduism Today*

"Like a Mother, Amma loves unconditionally and serves expediently."
— Comedian Russell Brand

"Amma has done more than many governments have done for their people."
— Nobel Peace Laureate Muhammad Yunus

"Truly a saint." — United Nations Partnerships

"This celestial being who walks among us!" — Author Wayne Dyer

"The darkness cannot compete with Her." — Actor Jim Carrey

"The embodiment of pure Love — Ammachi heals." — Author Deepak Chopra MD

www.ingramcontent.com/pod-product-compliance
Lightning Source LLC
Chambersburg PA
CBHW070530090426
42735CB00013B/2937